MADE FOR MORE

Curtis Martin

Nihil obstat: Mr. Francis X. Maier
               Censor Deputatus

Imprimatur: +Most Reverend Charles J. Chaput, O.F.M. Cap.
               Archbishop of Denver
               July 22, 2008

Published by Beacon Publishing
in agreement with EPIC Publishing,
a subsidiary of FOCUS
www.focusonline.org

For more information about this title and other books and CDs available through the Dynamic Catholic Book Program, please visit:
www.DynamicCatholic.com

Printed in the United States of America
ISBN 978-1-937509-16-3

CONTENTS

INTRODUCTION

I still haven't found what I'm looking for.
— U2

Not too long ago, I was asked to give a lecture on ethics at the University of Colorado. The question at hand was, "Is it ethical to buy a term paper online?" At first glance the question seems a bit silly, but as with many such questions, if you scratch the surface a bit, there might be something more significant waiting to be discovered.

I began the presentation by making an assumption. "I think most of us would agree that if we bought *all* of our term papers online, that would be unethical. But let's take a look at the hard case. Imagine that you have never bought a term paper, never cheated on an exam, and you are weeks away from graduating. It is just before final exams, and term papers are due. You have three major papers due all in the same week. Some unexpected circumstances arise and, despite your best efforts, you can get only two of the three papers done. If you don't get the third paper in, you will fail the course. If you fail the course, you will not be able to graduate. What then? Would it be all right to go online and buy a term paper?"

I gave them a few minutes to ponder the issue. Nobody spoke.

"Let me ask you this. 'Why would you *want* to buy the term paper?'"

I waited for a response. After a few moments one brave soul spoke up: "Because I want to pass the class."

I responded, "That's a very good reason. Why do you want to pass the course?"

Another pause and then someone else said, "Because I want to graduate."

I replied, "That is a really good motivation. Graduating from college is a noble goal. So why do you want to graduate?"

A third voice came from the crowd. "Because a college degree is an important part of a solid resume."

"A solid resume, seems like a good thing. Why do you want one?"

"Because I want to get a good job."

"Great! A good job is a really good thing. Why do you want one?"

"Because I want to make a lot of money."

There were a few chuckles from the audience, but I pressed on and encouraged them: "Money is a really good thing. Why do you want a lot of money?"

"Because I want to buy nice things."

"Makes sense to me. But why do you want nice things?"

"Because I want to be happy."

I smiled and waited for a few seconds. This answer was a bit different from all the others. Each of the previous responses referenced a means to an end, a way of getting something greater. Happiness is different; it is the *reason* we act. If you think about it, happiness is almost always why we do what we do. We *want* to be happy; it is as though we were *made* for happiness.

I went back and reviewed the answers we had gathered with the students. We had walked through a series of steps that lead to happiness. But was each of these steps really the best way to achieve happiness? Passing a class, graduating, building a resume, getting a job, making money, and acquiring things all seem to be good in themselves. But what about our first step? It seemed that cheating had been the first step toward happiness, but had it really been a step in the right direction? Does cheating *lead* to happiness? No, having to look at myself in the mirror and admit that I am a cheater does not bring me joy.

If becoming a cheater is not the source of true happiness, then it is unethical to buy a term paper, because ethics is all about doing what is right so that we can cultivate authentic happiness. Ethics and morality are not intended as rules just to keep us in line; they are guides to lead us towards happiness.

What could be better than lasting happiness? Judging from

our behavior, nothing. That's because all our choices—including the evil ones—are ultimately aimed at getting happiness. Some people don't believe this, but it's true. We cannot *not* will our own happiness. We can only choose right or wrong ways of gaining it. Many of our choices deliver only temporary or fleeting happiness, sometimes at the cost of our ultimate happiness. Good choices offer a lasting, deeper kind of happiness. And only one thing is better than lasting happiness: everlasting happiness.

But *is* there such a thing as everlasting happiness? Could it be that the happiness we experience in this world is not the main event but merely a foretaste of something more? Suppose the principal purpose of this world is to prepare us for eternal happiness. If we are creatures made for another world, that would certainly explain why we seem to long for so much more than what this world offers. But this raises a potential question: What if you died and found out that there was indeed a heaven but you were not going? Talk about cosmic failure! No amount of earthly success can counterbalance the failure to gain eternal life. If there is a heaven, what earthly good would you be willing to exchange to gain this everlasting prize?

A Worthy Reflection

I think it's worth a few minutes' thought to consider what eternal life might be like. Imagine, if you will, that you die today and find yourself at the gates of heaven. In the twinkling of an eye, the great mystery of whether there is life after death is over!

Yes, there is indeed a heaven, and it is just on the other side of those gates. All that matters now is whether you are in or out. To your everlasting happiness, you are invited in!

The pearly gates open, and you walk into a breathtaking banquet hall that is at once as majestic and spacious as the Rocky Mountains, as beautiful as the Louvre, and as welcoming as your grandmother's kitchen. The moment you arrive, the only appropriate response is tears of unimaginable joy. The joy you experience is more than that of a new mother when her baby is first handed to her in the delivery room, or of a father when he first sees his daughter in her wedding dress, or of an athlete when his team has finally won a championship after years of struggle. The beauty of the place satisfies every fiber of your being.

Heaven is packed with millions upon millions of people having the time of their (eternal) lives, yet somehow it never feels crowded or congested. To your great joy, you are reunited with your family and friends who have gone before you. While you have so much to say to one another, there is no rush—you have all of eternity. You realize that nothing wonderful you ever experienced on earth even comes close to the intensity of this new joy—a joy you know will never end.

You sigh with contentment. Not a temporary contentment. A *permanent* contentment. Not just an "all my troubles are over" contentment, but an *all trouble is over* contentment. This is quite literally the best day of your life. Sure, it may not have started out so well—with dying and all—but talk about landing on your feet!

All of a sudden, the lights flash a couple of times to signal that it is time to be seated at the heavenly banquet. You look around quickly, not quite knowing what to do—after all, it's your first day. Finally, you spy a single open chair at a nearby table. A beautiful name tag is resting near the plate, and it has your name on it, so you casually sit down. The white tablecloth seems to glow.

Everyone is engaged in lively conversation. You want to ease into one of the discussions, so you calmly turn to the man on your left, but he is speaking with someone on his other side. The woman to your right is also busy chatting with somebody. Then you notice a robust-looking gentleman sitting directly across the table, and he isn't speaking with anyone. You discreetly give a little wave to catch his eye and say, "Hello, it is my first day here. Who are you?" He smiles and responds, "I am Bishop Ignatius." You are thinking, "Wow! My first day, and I'm speaking to a bishop!"

Just then the person to his side says, "The bishop is being humble. He is actually *Saint* Ignatius of Antioch, one of the early Church Fathers." You try not to let your jaw drop, but this is pretty amazing: not just a bishop, but a saint! What are the odds? Then you think, *Wait a minute! This is heaven. Everybody here is a saint!*

As you mull this over, you notice that your new friend seems to be waiting for you to say something. Your mind races. *What should I say to someone like this?* You pause a moment and then blurt out the first thing that comes into your mind. "So ... Bishop, can you tell me a little about yourself?"

St. Ignatius looks thoughtfully at you for a moment, smiles, and begins. "I had a blessed life. You know that at the end of Jesus' life, after his death and resurrection, he taught his disciples for forty days. On his very last day on earth, Ascension Thursday, he commissioned them, saying:

> All authority in heaven and earth has been given to me. Go therefore and make disciples of all nations, baptizing them in the name of the Father and of the Son and of the Holy Spirit, teaching them to observe all that I have commanded you; and behold, I am with you always, to the close of the age. (Mt 28:18-20)

"Just after he spoke these words, Jesus was taken up into heaven. The disciples who were there took Jesus seriously and went out and did just as he had said. One of those disciples was the apostle John, and I was one of the disciples *he* made."

You sit up with a start. This guy is older than his youthful, glorified body makes him appear!

"You knew St. John the apostle?!"

The bishop smiles. "Knew him? Yes." Ignatius falls silent for a moment as he collects his thoughts. Then he continues, "Life with St. John was amazing. He had been completely transformed by the Savior. His relationship with our risen Lord had changed everything in his life. I remember when he was exiled to the island of Patmos. The memory is as clear for me as the day I was made the bishop of Antioch, where the followers of Jesus were first called Christians."

Ignatius continues to tell us about how the Church grew and how many more lives were changed by their encounter with the risen Jesus. He reminisces about the eventual persecution that arose and how the Romans arrested him and led him in chains across Asia Minor and Europe back to Rome, where he was tried for crimes against the state and for promoting this new religion.

At this point, a young man sitting near Ignatius interjects. "I remember the letters you wrote!" The young man turns to you and explains that, as Ignatius was marched under guard from Antioch (in modern-day Turkey) to Rome, he wrote letters to the young churches encouraging them to remain strong in the faith and asking them not to try to prevent him from meeting his death. The young man closes his eyes and recites Ignatius' words back to him from memory:

> I enjoin all, that I am dying willingly for God's sake, if only you do not prevent it. I beg you, do not do me an untimely kindness. Allow me to be

eaten by the beasts, which are my way of reaching
to God. I am God's wheat, and I am to be ground
by the teeth of wild beasts, so that I may become
the pure bread of Christ. (*Epistle to the Romans*, 4)

He opens his eyes and looks at Ignatius. "It's the letter
you wrote to the Christians in Rome," he adds. "I have never
forgotten those words since the day that letter was first read to
me! I've always wanted to thank you for your courage!"

Ignatius is quiet and gracious, you think. *He doesn't seem especially
interested in himself.* Meanwhile, you begin to realize how strange
and wonderful your companions are. After a pause, you ask, "So
what happened?"

Ignatius says simply, "They brought me to trial, I was found
guilty of being a Christian, and they fed me to the wild beasts
... I have been here ever since. I owe it all to God."

There is a long pause, and then St. Ignatius of Antioch
turns to you and says, "So, please, tell me your story..."

It is amazing how eternity affects your perspective. You are
not sure what you would say about your life but you might say
something like this:

"Wow! If only I knew when I was young what I can now
see so clearly: that heaven is not disconnected from earth. My life
was given to me as a gift—a dramatic adventure! All too often,
I ignored the reality of heaven and lived on earth as though

the things of the world were all that mattered. But heaven has a funny way of putting everything into its proper perspective. Here in heaven, I am surrounded by people who let God live within them and through them. In their very lives they gave glory to God, and now, his very life in us is the cause of our joy and the glory of God himself!"

"Yes!" interjects a bald man seated on the other side of the table, about four chairs away, who knocks over a wine glass in his excitement. It's St. Bonaventure. He cries, "The world was made for the glory of God, not to increase his glory, but to show it forth and to communicate it! Creatures came into existence when the key of love opened his hand."[1]

Then, from a few seats down the table, the Oxford professor and Christian author C.S. Lewis, overhearing our conversation, hoists his glass and cries, "It's like I always said, 'If heaven and hell exist, nothing else matters; if heaven and hell *don't* exist, then nothing matters.'"

Of course, before we get to heaven and find our heart's deepest longing fulfilled, it is only reasonable to ask, "Is there a God? Is there really a heaven?"

There are only two possible answers to these questions: yes or no. We can live as though heaven and hell don't exist, or we can live as though they do. But if we are not quite convinced,

---

[1] St. Bonaventure, *In II Sent.* I,2,2,1.; St. Thomas Aquinas, *Sent. 2,* Prol.; see *Catechism of the Catholic Church,* 293

it makes much more sense to live as though they do. Think about what is at stake. If we choose to live as though there *is* a heaven and a hell and we are wrong, we have lost nothing—at death, it's lights out. But, if we choose to live as though there is *no* heaven or hell and we are wrong, one day we might well find ourselves at the beginning of our eternal destiny only to realize too late that, by failing to pursue heaven, we have lost it forever. As author Albert Camus said: "I would rather live my life as if there is a God and die to find out there isn't, than live my life as if there isn't and die to find out there is."

The rest of this book is dedicated to examining the compelling evidence God has given us that he does indeed exist and that there *is* a heaven. This evidence is not a theory or a legal argument: it is a *person*. If we want to examine the evidence for heaven, the best place to start is with the historical person known as Jesus of Nazareth. In his life, teachings, death, and resurrection, he shows us that we have been created to live a life of greatness here on earth and to live in everlasting happiness while giving him glory forever. If we let him, he will help us discover the real story of the adventure of our life—that we were made for more. For his revelation is the drama of the soul's choice.

CHAPTER 1

WHO DO *YOU* SAY THAT I AM?

For a moment, forget what you know—or think you know—about religion in general and Christianity in particular. Let's take an impartial look at the life of Jesus of Nazareth and begin with a plain fact: Throughout the entire world and all of history, it would be hard to find any individual whose life has had a greater impact than that of Jesus. One need not be a Christian to say this. H.G. Wells, no particular fan of Christianity, wrote:

> I am an historian, I am not a believer, but I must confess as an historian that this penniless preacher from Nazareth is irrevocably the very center of history. Jesus Christ is easily the most dominant figure in all history.

The impact of Jesus is quite amazing when we recall that he lived 2,000 years ago in a backwater of the Roman Empire and never traveled far from home (except when he lived in Egypt for a short time as a child). He never held political office, never wrote a book, never invented something, never discovered anything, never led an army into battle and never amassed great wealth. In fact, he never did any of the things that are typically considered "historic."

We know almost nothing about ninety percent of his brief thirty-three years on earth, and during the three short years of his public work, he spent much of his time in out-of-the-way villages rather than in the one city of influence in the region, Jerusalem. The evidence indicates that he seemed to avoid publicity, even commanding his followers not to tell anyone of the extraordinary miracles he was said to have performed. Indeed, the one act for which he is most remembered—and the one thing to which the eyewitnesses of his life devote the most ink in their documents about him—is that, by all conventional standards, he died as a spectacular failure, rejected by the very people he sought, in a particularly gruesome and shameful way reserved for the lowest dregs of society. He appeared to be such a failure, in fact, that his body had to be placed in somebody else's tomb.

How is it, then, that Jesus has become the single most influential person in the history of the world? Not only do Christians follow him as their savior, but other religions regard him as a holy man. Cultures and religious traditions have been deeply impacted by the civilization that spread throughout the world in his name. Even people of no religious faith have been profoundly influenced by him, such that, in the West, to be an atheist means primarily to disbelieve in Jesus. It is not Zeus, Quetzalcoatl, or Moloch that a typical Western atheist busies himself with not believing in.

Even the calendar most of the world uses today records time from the birth of Jesus of Nazareth. "A.D." is an abbreviation for *in anno Domini,* which is Latin for "in the year of our Lord."

So what sets this man apart from the billions of others who have lived upon this earth? Many people have lived longer lives and many seem to have accomplished far greater things. Why would a man who died in the prime of his life—naked, penniless, shamed, virtually alone, and in great agony—become the focal point of history?

Paradoxically, it is precisely at this moment of seeming failure—the shameful death of Jesus—that we can start trying to unlock the mystery. Why would a man who "went about doing good and healing all that were oppressed" (Acts 10:38), be rejected, tortured, and killed? What exactly did Jesus do to earn such a fate?

The documents from the period closest to him describe him as "a sign of contradiction" (Lk 2:34). At first glance Jesus may appear to be like other religious figures, preaching love of neighbor; reminding us of the permanent things that all prophets, poets, and storytellers have called us to contemplate; and urging people to turn toward God and to love one another. But something separates Jesus from all the others.

The primary message of Jesus is not a call to moral perfection, although that is an element of his teaching. No, the primary message of Jesus is *Jesus*. Other religious leaders like Moses, Buddha, Mohammed, and Confucius had a message about God or right living for their followers. But the most they had to say about themselves was that they were teachers of the true and right way or a prophet of God.

Jesus departs from all the religious leaders of the world by making a far more radical and unique claim. He claims not to be a messenger but to be the Message. In short, his identity is the issue.

So who *is* he? That question—perhaps the most provocative question in the history of the whole human race—is one he himself put to his followers: "Who do men say that the Son of Man is?" (Mt 16:13).

His followers' answers were varied: Some people said John the Baptist, and others Jeremiah or one of the prophets. And, like his followers, we may be tempted to leave that question in the realm of public opinion—what do others think? But Jesus won't let us stay in the abstract. He requires of each of us the same thing he demanded of the apostles: to make a personal choice. "Who do *you* say that I am?"

Your answer to this question may involve some deep consideration, but the potential answers are surprisingly limited.

Let's look at some of the non-Christian attempts to explain Jesus.

A Moral Teacher Like No Other?

One very popular attempt to explain Jesus is to see him as a great sage. Now, to be sure, he is a wise man standing in a long tradition of wise men. Many religious figures in history passed on wise sayings, did good, and proclaimed justice. Unlike theirs, Jesus' teachings possess a clarity and a curiously counterintuitive quality that speak of one who operated at a radically different level. He was "quick on his feet" in debate, but he was much more than a snappy debater. He thought deeply and, more importantly, he lived deeply.

Even those who do not believe in Jesus find his teachings compelling. For instance, the great scientist Albert Einstein said:

> As a child I received instruction both in the Bible and in the Talmud. I am a Jew, but I am enthralled by the luminous figure of the Nazarene ... No one can read the Gospels without feeling the actual presence of Jesus. His personality pulsates in every word. No myth is filled with such life.[2]

And yet, for all that, we miss the point almost entirely if we treat him merely as a wise man. Why? Because again and again Jesus is recorded making claims that no mere wise man ever made.

---

[2] "What Life Means to Einstein: An Interview by George Sylvester Viereck," *The Saturday Evening Post,* October 29, 1926.

Jesus Forgives Sins

In just one of many similar incidents, Jesus is brought a paralyzed man and, when he sees the faith of the man's companions, he tells the man, "Your sins are forgiven" (see Mt 9:2-7). The people are scandalized. They ask, "Who can forgive sins but God?" Then Jesus asks, "Which is easier: to forgive sins or say, 'Rise and walk'? But so that you may know that the Son of Man has authority to forgive sins…" he turned to the paralytic and said, "Rise, take up your mat, and go home." As the man stood for the first time, his restored body gave physical witness to the forgiveness Jesus had granted.

Two thousand years of taking the Christian revelation for granted can dull our appreciation of what is meant by Jesus' act of forgiving a man's sins. Jesus is not saying "niceness is nice." Nor is he trying to make a disabled person feel better about himself. Rather, as his critics understood perfectly, he was claiming to be the One offended by all sins. He did not forgive someone who had tried to harm him, as we might forgive a reckless driver who cuts in front of us or an acquaintance who rifles through our wallet. He offered forgiveness to a man who was, humanly speaking, a perfect stranger. To do that was, as his critics knew all too well, a claim to be God—because it was a claim to be the One chiefly offended by human sins.

The real miracle, then, is not the physical healing of the paralytic, but the actual forgiveness of his sins. For Jesus is, by that act, claiming to be God. His critics are right: only God can forgive sins, and Jesus does not dispute that. He heals the man precisely to drive home the point that he, the Son of Man, is also the Son of God.

Jesus Claims Preexistence

In John 8, the religious leaders criticize Jesus, saying, "Who do you think you are? Do you think you are better than Abraham?" Jesus responds, "Truly, truly I say to you, before Abraham was, I am" (Jn 8:58). Again, a modern reader may not get the immensity of what is being claimed here. Jesus is not merely claiming to be older than Abraham (who died about two thousand years before Jesus was born). That would be extraordinary enough. Jesus is saying infinitely more. "I AM" is the Name of God in Hebrew, the Name by which he revealed himself to Moses in Exodus 3. It is a Name so sacred that Jews do not even write or speak it. Jesus, in this passage, takes that Name to himself! He is claiming to be the same eternal God who spoke to Moses in the burning bush! The religious leaders understand his claim perfectly. That is why they pick up stones and try to kill him as a blasphemer.

Here are some other key things Jesus did:

Jesus Claims to Be the Only Way to the Father

Like all sages, Jesus shows us a way to become a better person. He guides us, both by word and example, to be more loving;

to care for the weak, the sick, and the poor; and to forgive the unforgivable. But far more than *showing* us the way, Jesus says, "*I am* the way, and the truth, and the life; no one comes to the Father but by me" (Jn 14:6). This statement, if not true, would make Jesus an egomaniac, not a good man. On the other hand, if Jesus' claim is true, then he is claiming to be much more than a "good man."

Jesus Allows Himself to be Worshipped

In John 20:26-29, we find Jesus and the apostles together a week after his resurrection. The apostle Thomas had not been present the week before when Jesus appeared to the others. Thomas had made it clear that he would not believe that Jesus had indeed risen from the dead unless he could stick his fingers into the wounds of Jesus. Then Jesus suddenly appears and Thomas falls to the ground, saying, "My Lord and my God!" Being strict Jews, Jesus and the apostles were necessarily monotheists, worshipping only one God. Yet when Thomas exclaims, "My Lord and my God," neither Jesus nor the other apostles correct him. Instead, Jesus accepts this worship, thereby claiming again to *be* that one God of Israel. The more you look, the clearer it becomes: no one thought Jesus was just a sage.

A Guru?

Once we really grasp what Jesus says about himself, the sheer magnitude of the claim can often make it irresistible to find some way to dodge it, because the implications are so huge for us. So if Jesus is not a sage, some people will attempt to solve the problem by turning to Eastern religions. Maybe Jesus was the "guru to the Jews." According to this theory, Jesus' claims to be God are taken in a vaguely Hindu sense. "Yes," goes this line of reasoning, "Jesus did claim to be God, but that is because he believed that everything is God and he was trying to awaken us to the God-consciousness of which we are all a part. So he claimed to be God, but he also believed that every person, and indeed every *thing,* is God."

The main problem with this account is that it simply doesn't match the record in the least. Jesus gives not the slightest hint of the Hindu pantheistic mindset. He rather emphatically teaches that he is God and we are not. He emphasizes that he is from above and we are from below (Jn 8:23), that we are sinners (Mt 7:11) and he is without sin (Jn 8:46), that God is one, and that the earth is God's footstool, not a cosmic extension of his divinity (Mt 5:34). In fact, Jesus is thoroughly Jewish with a thoroughly Jewish conception of a God who is utterly distinct from his creation. The God he claims to be is not Vishnu, Brahma, or any other pagan deity. He calls himself by the Name of the God of Israel—I AM.

Either God or a Bad Man

Jesus claims to be much more than merely a good man. And

if he is not who he claims to be, then he cannot be a good man. In his book *Mere Christianity*, the great Christian apologist C.S. Lewis describes this *trilemma*.

Jesus claims to be God, so either he is God or he is not. If he's not God, then we are left with two options: he either knows that he is not God and is a liar, or he mistakenly thinks he is God and is a lunatic. The one thing he most certainly is not is merely a good man.

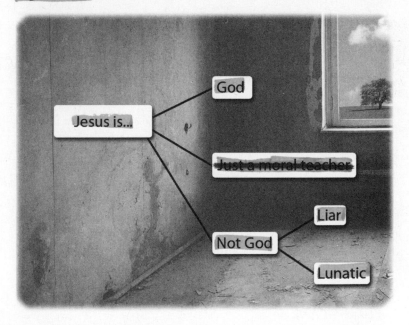

If Jesus is a liar, he is not just any ordinary liar. He is a liar of, well, biblical proportions because he tricks many into thinking that he is telling the truth by working miracles. He would have to be a spectacular liar, as his claims are not just little fibs but lies of unprecedented magnitude about the most important thing imaginable. For a man to make and seriously sustain such a claim to innocent people, he would have to be far more than a mere "hoaxster." He would have to be deeply evil.

Yet accounting for Jesus as evil is preposterous. In his teachings and, far more, in his actions he lives a life that is utterly oriented toward "bear[ing] witness to the truth," as he puts it (Jn 18:37). If he is a liar, then for what conceivable purpose? Liars lie in the pursuit of some gain. What does Jesus gain as a result of his claims? Earthly power? When they try to crown him, he runs away. Status? He only wins the fleeting admiration of a small crowd of seemingly unimportant people—prostitutes, tax collectors, fishermen—and the undying enmity of the leaders who are bent on his destruction and who have the means to accomplish it. When he is on trial for his life and is challenged point-blank to answer whether he is indeed the Christ, the Son of God, he does not hedge and fib. He answers, again in language pregnant with double meaning, "I AM" (Lk 22:70)—thereby inviting crucifixion and the most horrific and shameful death known to antiquity. No liar bent on earthly gain would do this.

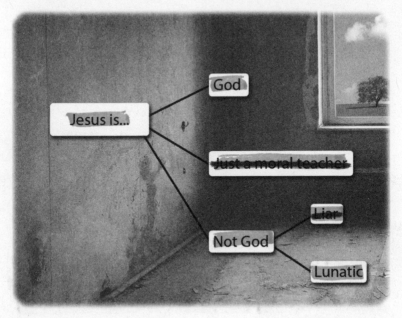

So if Jesus claims to be God and is not, we are left with only one alternative: he is insane. The trouble is that he is radically unlike any other lunatic who has ever claimed to be God. Read the Sermon on the Mount in Matthew 5–7. Does that sound like the manifesto of a psychotic to you? Watch his clever interactions with his enemies or his warm conversations with his friends. Do you think, "Here is a deranged man"?

On the contrary, it begins to look as though the difficulty of accounting for Jesus in any way but the way Peter did is indeed very great. And Peter's answer to Jesus' question is heart-stopping: "You are the Christ, the Son of the living God" (Mt 16:16).

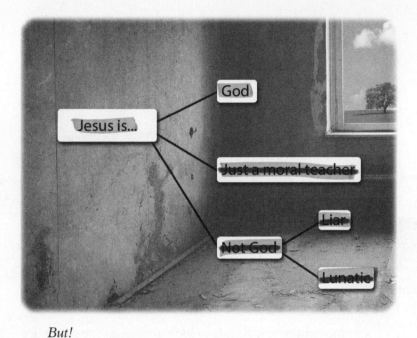

But!

"Yes," says the skeptic, "*if* you believe everything you read. But why should we trust the story the Bible tells us?"

I'll tell you why.

CHAPTER 2

CAN YOU BELIEVE WHAT YOU READ?

The biblical evidence about Jesus, if accurate, is compelling. But can we believe what we read? How do we know that what the New Testament claims about Jesus actually occurred? The book was written a long time ago, and many therefore conclude that it is filled with contradictions and historical inaccuracies. But is it? Others charge that, even if the New Testament we have today really preserves what the eyewitnesses claim to have seen, it is still only the official air-brushed story of the Church, written to make the apostles look good.

Some Red Herrings

Before we can discuss the accuracy of the New Testament, we have to deal with a few modern prejudices that leave many people unable to evaluate the text fairly in the same way they might evaluate the text of some other ancient book like, say, Plato's *Republic*. Here are some of the stumbling blocks critical readers of the Bible bring up. Let's see how to properly approach and address these challenges:

1)   Mistaking "Complementary" for "Contradictory"

In Matthew 5:1, Matthew tells us that Jesus went up on the mountain and preached the Sermon on the Mount. In Luke 6:17, we are told that Jesus stood on a level place (i.e, the plain) and gave a sermon that sounds much like the Sermon on the Mount. Was Jesus on a mountain or a plain? Is this a contradiction? No. Just as many modern speakers give the same talk in different locations, Jesus would have restated this sermon many times because it represents the core of his teachings. Matthew recalls Jesus' sermon as it was given on the mountain because Matthew is highlighting how Jesus is the New Moses delivering a New Law on a New Mountain. Luke introduces it on a plain because Luke is placing emphasis on Jesus as the new Adam who makes salvation available to all, not merely to a small elite. In reality, Jesus is the fulfillment of both Moses and Adam. Each author is highlighting the complementary aspects of Jesus' life by drawing from the superabundance of real events that actually took place. The ability to distinguish between "complementary" and "contradictory" is essential to reading the historical accounts.

2)   Ignorance of Literary Form

Many people today subscribe to the notion that if the Bible is not a newspaper account, it is devoid of truth. In fact, however, truth is told in many different forms and genres of literature, and the Bible contains all of them. To interpret a passage from the Bible properly, we must understand the *literary form* of that particular passage. For example, in the gospels, Jesus makes use of many *parables.* A correct understanding is to affirm that Jesus actually spoke these parables. It is not necessary, however, to believe that there was a historical Good Samaritan or Prodigal Son, only that Jesus used these fictional stories to teach truths about charity, mercy, and the love of God.

In addition, Jesus used *hyperbole*, a form of literary exaggeration. For example, he tells us in Matthew 5:30 that if your right hand causes you to sin, you should cut it off. While our hands may be used to *commit* sin, they cannot *cause* us to sin. Sin comes from the heart, so the remedy for sin is not literal, physical amputation. Jesus is using a figure of speech to convey a sense of urgency in renouncing sin.

Moderns tend to say, "The Bible is full of poetic truths, but you should never take it literally." The problem with this approach is it misses the point that some parts are *meant* to be taken literally. When it says that Jesus was born in Bethlehem of Judea or that the women came to the tomb of Jesus on the third day, found it empty, and met the Risen Christ, this is meant to be understood not in some vague "poetic sense" but in a literal way. We ought to always read the Bible "literarily" and, when appropriate, take it literally as well.

3) Biblical Use of Non-Technical Language

The New Testament uses non-technical and pre-modern language. That does not mean it is unreliable. For example,

the gospels tell us the women came to the tomb at "sunrise."
Is the mention of "sunrise" made because the gospel writers
are trying to assert the technical details of the ancient theory
that the sun revolves around the earth? No, it's done for
the same reason that you might say, "I'm going fishing at
sunrise." The gospel writers are using human language in
a human way. We all talk in this way. Trying to demand
that an ancient text conform to unreasonable expectations
inevitably leads to misinterpretation and confusion.

4) Failure to Read in Context

We need to be very careful that we read a biblical text in
its proper context. The devil himself quotes scripture, out of
context, to tempt Jesus (Mt 4:5-6). Without proper context,
any text can be twisted to say almost anything. For example,
in Matthew 27:5 we read that Judas "hanged himself." And
in Luke 10:37 we are told, "Go and do likewise." If we pull
these two passages out of context and combine them, we
read, "Judas hanged himself: go and do likewise." But the
Bible does not teach us to commit suicide. Understanding
context helps us to interpret the texts properly.

5) Resistance to the Unexplained

Finally, just because something is *unexplained* doesn't
necessarily mean that it's *impossible*. Just because we do not
understand something in the Bible does not mean that the Bible

is wrong. Until the last generation, there was some debate among scientists as to how exactly bumblebees could fly. The laws of aerodynamics could not explain how they could fly given the relatively small size of their wings in relation to their body. Yet bumblebees kept flying. In the same way, we read certain things in the Bible (such as the resurrection of Jesus) and do not understand how such things could be. The authors of the New Testament didn't know how such a thing could be; they just knew that it had, in fact, occurred.

Similarly, to say that "ancient people believed in Jesus' resurrection because they were ignorant of science" is simply not true. People have *always* known perfectly well that dead men do not come back to life and do not need a guy in a white lab coat to tell them that. Appeals to science in declaring miracles "impossible" miss the point. Science, by definition, can speak only to measurable events in this universe. It cannot state whether a God who exists outside this universe might intervene in the created order, any more than a constitutional scholar can declare that, in his expert opinion, it is impossible for there ever to be a revolution that might suspend, alter, or abolish the United States Constitution.

Textual Criticism

There is a scholarly discipline called *textual criticism* that deals with the reliability of ancient texts. The focus of this discipline is: Can we trust that what we read is an accurate reflection of what was originally written? It is a discipline that deals with all books in the same manner and pays no heed to claims of inspiration. It deals with the text of the New Testament just as it would the text of Julius Caesar's record of the war in Gaul—impartially and objectively.

There are three basic types of evidence used in testing the reliability of any ancient text: bibliographic, internal, and external.

Bibliographic Evidence

One common argument against trusting the New Testament is that we do not have any of the original manuscripts, so why trust the versions we have today?

The problem with this approach is that it virtually eliminates all our knowledge of the pre-modern world if we press the argument very hard. For no original manuscript of any writing until very near the modern era has survived. Most ancient documents were written on papyrus, which decayed over time, so it was necessary to make copies. If we make the existence of an original manuscript our sole criterion for trusting a document, then we must scrap almost everything we know of history before a century or two ago.

Happily, we are not bound by such a rigorous approach. For it is possible to provide powerful evidence that our modern versions correspond to the original. To see how this works, let's look at a couple of other ancient texts.

Demosthenes was a Greek orator who wrote in the year 300 B.C. We do not have any originals of his work, but we have eight copies dating from A.D. 1100. All of the other copies of Demosthenes that have been made over the intervening centuries are based upon those ancient eight.

Julius Caesar's *Gallic Wars* was written about a century before the New Testament and, like the New Testament, we have no originals in Caesar's hand. Indeed, only ten ancient copies of the text exist, dating from A.D. 900. So how do we know they are accurate representations of what Caesar wrote?

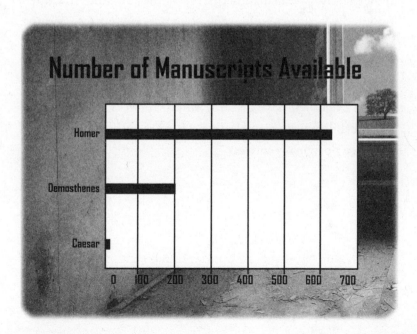

We are able to test the accuracy and reliability of ancient manuscripts in a number of ways. First, we do so by comparing the copies of ancient manuscripts to one another. As a general rule, when a copying error occurs, it occurs in one manuscript. If one manuscript varies from the other extant manuscripts, the discrepancy will usually be obvious.

In addition, other ancient authors quote from the original source we no longer possess. For instance, our oldest complete manuscript of Matthew dates from the fourth century. But Jerome, a biblical scholar who lived in the fourth century, tells us he saw the *original* manuscript of Matthew, dating back three hundred years further than the copy we now possess. Jerome then goes on to translate Matthew into Latin, which means we have access to Jerome's knowledge of Matthew. When an ancient witness to a document (such as Jerome) and our manuscript(s) of that document say the same thing, there is a high degree of probability that we are seeing what the author (in this case, Matthew) originally wrote.

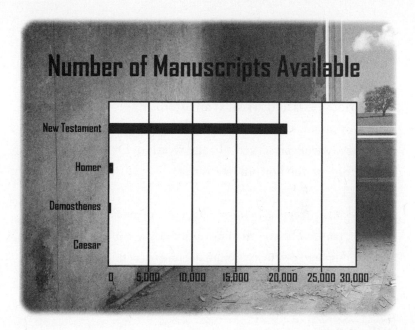

Compare and Contrast Non-Christian Texts with the New Testament

When it comes to the New Testament, we possess not a tiny handful of manuscripts and fragments, but *5,366* ancient manuscripts and fragments, all datable to within fifty to one hundred years of the originals.[3] And this number doesn't include the translations of the text from the original Greek into other languages. We have more than 10,000 copies of the Latin Vulgate, the translation of the Bible made by St. Jerome in the fourth century, often from manuscripts that no longer exist. We

---

[3] *The New Evidence That Demands a Verdict*, Josh McDowell (Nashville: Nelson, 1999) p.38

have more than 2,000 copies in Coptic and over 4,000 in Slavic languages.

That is a lot of data with which to compare and contrast the various texts and arrive at an astonishingly high degree of accuracy about what the original Greek text actually said (and it is already well-preserved). In the words of Dr. John Warwick Montgomery, the bottom line is this:

> To be skeptical of the resultant text of the New Testament books is to allow all of classic antiquity to slip into obscurity. For no documents of the ancient period are as well attested bibliographically as the New Testament.[4]

Sacredness Only Raises the Stakes

The thing about sacred texts is that people are far more likely to exhibit enormous care with them precisely *because* they are sacred. The astounding precision of the biblical copyists is a case in point. The copyists took painstaking care to keep the text faithful to the one from which they were copied. Early Christians would copy word for word and then have other people examine their work. The number of letters, words, and lines were counted. If even the slightest error was found, they would destroy the copy and start over again rather than risk the sacrilege of corrupting the sacred text.

---

[4] McDowell, p.36

The result of this rigor was impressive: Biblical reliability and fidelity to the original text have been scientifically established by textual criticism. Not a single Christian doctrine is placed in doubt because of any question concerning the reliability of the Bible—and certainly nothing that throws the slightest shadow on the crystal-clear claims of the deity of Jesus Christ found in the New Testament.

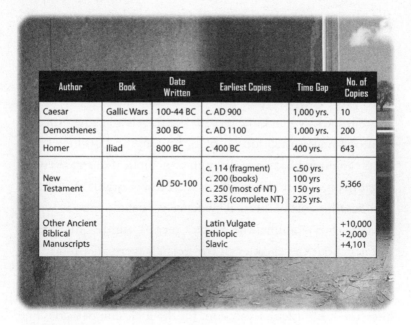

Author	Book	Date Written	Earliest Copies	Time Gap	No. of Copies
Caesar	Gallic Wars	100-44 BC	c. AD 900	1,000 yrs.	10
Demosthenes		300 BC	c. AD 1100	1,000 yrs.	200
Homer	Iliad	800 BC	c. 400 BC	400 yrs.	643
New Testament		AD 50-100	c. 114 (fragment) c. 200 (books) c. 250 (most of NT) c. 325 (complete NT)	c.50 yrs. 100 yrs 150 yrs 225 yrs.	5,366
Other Ancient Biblical Manuscripts			Latin Vulgate Ethiopic Slavic		+10,000 +2,000 +4,101

Internal Evidence

The second test for reliability is *internal evidence*. Does the document itself stand on its own? Does it contradict itself? Is it logical and plausible?

For instance, if a text gives us obviously wrong information about the customs, persons, or geography of first century Judea, that would be evidence against reliability. On the other hand, if a document purporting to be from John the Apostle records in an off-hand manner details that would likely be unknown to a later forger, this would be strong evidence that the author is indeed giving us an eyewitness account. So when John speaks in the present tense of architectural features in Jerusalem that did not survive the destruction of the Temple in A.D. 70, the most likely explanation is that the author was personally familiar with them—and therefore was a witness writing of things he saw. This helps us establish the date of a document.

Similarly, when Luke records the travels and adventures of Paul, he makes mention of various people and events. These facts can often be known through non-biblical sources as well. That helps us date the events in the New Testament.

Another sort of internal evidence is "details nobody would invent." For example, the gospels record highly unflattering details about the apostles. If the gospels were an air-brushed record designed to inflate Jesus into a god and his friends into his reliable witnesses, they would not contain many of the details they do. It is difficult to account for the inclusion of stories like Peter's denial of Jesus or the cowardice of the apostles. If the New Testament is merely the creation of the apostles, falsely claiming that Jesus was God, these inconvenient truths would be the first to go. Yet there they are.

A third kind of internal evidence is the "accidental" corroboration of widely dispersed sources.

External Evidence

The New Testament, of course, is written for everyone in every age, but it did have an initial audience. What did they think of it? How did they read it? This is the third aspect in determining not just the reliability of the biblical text, but also its meaning. What is the testimony of the original audience? Let's read the words of Irenaeus of Lyons (c. A.D. 180):

> So firm is the ground upon which these gospels rest
> that even the very heretics themselves bear witness
> to them and use them as a starting point for their
> endeavors to establish a certain doctrine.

Irenaeus' great teacher was a man named Polycarp. Polycarp's teacher was John the Apostle. When Polycarp was eighty-six years old, he was ordered to renounce Christ by the Roman authority. He refused, saying, "I have served Christ for six and eighty years, and never has he done me evil. How, then, can I blaspheme my King and Savior?"

Repeated many times by martyrs, this is a witness to the integrity of the apostles (who themselves all suffered or died for their testimonies) and, ultimately, to the integrity of the message they proclaim. The trustworthiness of the apostles is attested to by their decades of suffering, isolation, persecution, exile, ridicule, and death. The New Testament has likewise been tested more than any other text, and it has withstood the scrutiny of both friend and foe.

Conclusion

The New Testament record of Jesus' claims to deity are not myths or legends that slowly crept into the text over the course of centuries, corrupting a collection of writings about a nice rabbi and making him into a god. What we read in the New Testament today is what was written in the first century by eyewitnesses—or the eyewitnesses' companions. The simple fact is this: Jesus was not executed for saying, "love one another" or "try to be nice." He was executed for claiming to be the God of the universe—the I AM. He doesn't ask us merely to accept his *teachings*; he calls us to accept *him*. That is why he was executed. And that is why the apostles became the eyewitnesses to the greatest miracle in history: Jesus' resurrection from the dead.

CHAPTER 3

HE IS RISEN INDEED!

We have seen that Jesus stands alone in human history with his believable claim to be God. We have seen that the Bible provides a reliable record of his deeds and words— including the testimony to his miraculous works.

However, though the life of Jesus was truly extraordinary, it is what he did *after* his death that really sets him apart from all others: he rose from the dead. This was no Hollywood special effects trick; Jesus was really dead and he has truly risen. Centuries of Christian culture may have numbed us to this awe-inspiring fact, but the foundation of the entire Christian faith is the empty tomb. So let us consider it clearly. This event took place not in some mythological place, but in the very real city of Jerusalem at a very specific point in history, i.e., during the rule of the Roman procurator Pontius Pilate.

The entire Christian faith stands or falls with the resurrection of Jesus of Nazareth. For the heart of Christianity is not a series of principles or ideas; it is the person of Jesus Christ, raised bodily from death to glory at the right hand of the Father. St.

Paul echoes this very point when he writes to the Christians in Corinth: "If Christ has not been raised, then our preaching is in vain and your faith is in vain" (1 Cor 15:14).

The resurrection, in addition to being the ultimate proof of the claim of Christ, is also essential to each of us: Christ conquers death not only for himself but for all who believe in him. Being a Christian is not for the faint of heart; it is a radically dramatic response to the most radically dramatic event in all of history.

The resurrection is absolutely central to the preaching of the apostles. Very simply, the apostles have almost nothing else to say beyond "Jesus Christ, the Son of God, was raised from the dead for our salvation." That is the "good news." Without it, there would be no New Testament documents at all.

The authors of the New Testament get this news about the resurrection from Jesus himself before it even occurs—in his preaching. He hints at it in a cryptic remark to his foes in Jerusalem, "Destroy this temple, and in three days I will raise it up" (Jn 2:19).

Jesus becomes more clear about his coming resurrection immediately after bestowing the "keys of his kingdom" upon Peter when he declares to his disciples that he must go to Jerusalem and suffer many things from the elders, chief priests, and scribes, and be killed, and on the third day, raised (Mt 16:21).

All this drives home the fact that it was Jesus, not his followers, who believed in and predicted his resurrection. Indeed, again and again, the apostles remind us that they did not comprehend or believe what Jesus was saying about his resurrection. They were, in fact, scandalized by the cross and brokenhearted by Jesus' death. When he dies, we do not hear any of them saying, "That's okay. He's going to rise from the dead." When Jesus is crucified, his followers are traumatized; they flee and hide, not knowing what to do. It is only after he appears to them risen from the dead—and rebukes their lack of faith—that they begin to understand. And their preaching focuses entirely on the message that "this Jesus God raised up, and of that we all are witnesses" (Acts 2:32).

We must feel the weight of this absolutely extraordinary claim. In considering the resurrection, there are two facts we have to deal with: a missing corpse and reports of a risen Christ with a glorified body.

These facts, like the question "Who do you say I am?", admit a limited number of answers. Here are a few of the alternative theories that attempt to account for the empty tomb.

- Some, such as John Dominic Crossan of the Jesus Seminar, say Jesus wasn't buried in a tomb at all. They suggest that his body was thrown in a shallow grave and eaten by wild dogs. Then, delusional apostles consoled themselves with visions of a resurrection.

- Others, such as the late Kirsopp Lake, propose that the apostles went to the wrong tomb, found it empty, and, in some sort of mass hysteria, hallucinated a resurrection.

- Still others suggest that Jesus was raised "spiritually," that is, he was not raised bodily but was an apparition who made himself visible to the apostles to prove that he was still alive.

- Another theory holds that Jesus didn't really die on the cross; he just passed out. Later, he awoke in the tomb, pushed back the multi-ton rock, went out, and convinced his followers he had risen from the dead.

- Still others theorize that Jesus had a twin, who (depending on which theorist you listen to) either died in Jesus' place on the cross, or when Jesus died, said, "Now's my chance. My brother has been the popular one, but I can be the Messiah now." So the twin swept in and tricked the apostles into thinking he was Jesus. The Twin Theory is a popular idea among certain conspiracy theorists prone to listening to people like Michael Baigent, Richard Leigh, and Henry Lincoln, authors of *Holy Blood, Holy Grail.*

- Finally, another set of theories holds that someone stole Jesus' body.

Let's take a look at these desperate attempts to contradict the testimony of the apostles:

The Wild Dogs Theory

The problem with the "wild dogs" theory is twofold: 1) there is absolutely no evidence for it; and 2) there is plenty of evidence against it, including from Jesus' enemies. The actual records all say that the body of Jesus disappeared from the borrowed tomb of Joseph of Arimathea, a member of the ruling council of the Jews called the Sanhedrin. Joseph is not the sort of witness anybody would invent. He was well-known and could have easily refuted the claims if they were false.

In addition, even Jesus' enemies took the empty tomb for granted. They never denied that Jesus was buried in the tomb of Joseph of Arimathea. On the contrary, the first attempt to explain away the resurrection turns on their own decision to put a guard on the tomb. The story told by the opponents of the apostles is not "Jesus' corpse was eaten by wild dogs." It is that the apostles stole Jesus' body from Joseph's tomb while the guards slept. All of the evidence, even that given by Jesus' foes, points to Jesus' burial in the tomb of Joseph of Arimathea—a tomb empty on the third day.

The Wrong Tomb Theory

"OK," says the skeptic, "but what if the apostles went to the wrong tomb, found it empty, and hallucinated the resurrection."

This theory, however, presents us with the same problem as before. Jesus was buried in the tomb of a very prominent man who was known not only by the apostles but also by the Jewish and Roman leaders of the time. Even if the apostles were dumb enough to take a wrong turn, look in the wrong tomb, and immediately conclude that Jesus had risen from the dead, it is difficult to accept the notion that once they came back proclaiming Jesus' resurrection, nobody—including their enemies—would have gone to the right tomb and instantly produced Jesus' body.

A Word on Mass Hallucination

Both of the theories we have just discussed hold that the apostles were victims of some sort of mass hallucination. Yet hallucinations (much less mass hallucinations) require circumstances that were singularly lacking with the resurrection—for we do not find simple-minded apostles who were willing to believe anything after the death of Jesus. We find, instead, skeptical men who were slow to believe the testimony of the first witnesses who came from the tomb.

In addition, there is the problem of a mass hallucination in which nobody seems to recognize Jesus. The records tell us that, on three different occasions, Jesus appeared to his disciples and they did not even realize it was him.

The Spiritual Resurrection Theory

One way around the problems inherent in theories of mass hallucination is to say that the apostles really did see Jesus after his death, but that they witnessed merely a "spiritual resurrection" rather than a physical one. The problem with this theory is that a spiritual resurrection leaves the body of Jesus in the tomb. But as we have already seen, all of the evidence points to the fact that the tomb was empty. So Jesus' body must be accounted for. The way the apostles themselves account for it is quite clear:

> And [Jesus] said to them, "Why are you troubled, and why do questionings rise in your hearts? See my hands and my feet, that it is I myself; handle me, and see; for a spirit has not flesh and bones as you see that I have." And when he had said this, he showed them his hands and his feet. And while they still disbelieved for joy, and wondered, he said to them, "Have you anything here to eat?" They gave him a piece of broiled fish, and he took it and ate before them. (Lk 24:38-43)

The record of the eyewitnesses is clear: Jesus was raised bodily, not just spiritually.

The Swoon Theory

A perennial theory put forth to deal with the resurrection appearances of Jesus is that Jesus moved his own body from the tomb—because he wasn't dead. According to this theory, he merely passed out on the cross, either from his sufferings or from a drug he was given to fake his own death. This theory may satisfy people with little or no medical knowledge or critical thinking, but it's a tough sell otherwise.

Consider that Jesus, after a brutal scourging (a horrific punishment that often killed the victim before his execution could even be carried out), hung upon the cross for hours, gasping for breath and slowly undergoing the agonies of pericardial edema, a medical condition in which the heart and lungs fill with fluid until the victim suffocates. In addition to massive blood loss from the scourging, Jesus had large spikes driven directly through a major nerve trunk in his wrists. To breathe, he had to pull himself up by his wrists and push down on the nails through his feet. This would have gone on for *hours*.

To hurry along the process, the Roman soldiers, experts in death, decided to break his legs (so that he could not push himself up to catch his breath). In John 19:33, we read that the soldiers found that Jesus was already dead. Just to make sure, though, instead of breaking his legs, they pierced his side with a spear. Eyewitnesses saw blood and water gush from the wound. The modern medical term for this is "pericardial rupture." Even if the trained soldiers were wrong and Jesus was still alive, this thrust through the heart by a soldier's lance would have certainly killed him. We should also point out that none of his grieving followers and family noticed any signs of life as they prepared him for burial.

Let us, however, suppose that by some strange fluke, this man who had endured torture, scourging, crowning with thorns, a struggle through the streets of Jerusalem bearing the cross, crucifixion, a lance through the heart, and two nights and a day in a cold tomb in Jerusalem now regains consciousness—only to find a multi-ton stone blocking the entrance. Somehow, Jesus would have had to roll back the stone.

Then what? He would have staggered into town on bloody broken feet, suffering from shock, massive blood loss, disfiguring scars and hemorrhaging from his side—and instantly convinced his followers that he was the Conqueror of Death? The Swoon Theory illustrates just how far some people are willing to go to try to escape from the facts about Jesus.

The Missing Twin Theory

Still others try to explain away the resurrection with the theory of Jesus' "missing twin." Some cast the apostle Thomas in this role since his name means "twin." The problem is this: If Thomas died in Jesus' place, then how is it that he was present a week later with the apostles, demanding proof of Christ's resurrection as recorded in John 20? On the other hand, if Thomas posed as the risen Christ, then who was it that fell on his knees before Jesus and proclaimed, "My Lord and my God"? (Jn 20:28).

Faced with this obvious difficulty, some will claim that some unknown person was Jesus' twin. Either way, given the fact that there is absolutely no record of any such twin, how could this person have gone completely unnoticed by the apostles prior to this time? They had, after all, spent three years with Jesus and would have known his family very well. We also need to ask how this impostor passed through locked doors, vanished from sight in an instant, and completely and utterly vanished forty days later after faking his ascension into heaven (Acts 1). In short, to accept this theory, we have to claim that Jesus' twin pulled off the greatest hoax in history—and for what reason? What was the point of it all?

So we are back to the following conclusion: Jesus was dead—and yet the tomb in which he was buried was found empty. So if these crazy theories can't explain the empty tomb, the only other option is that someone must have taken his body. But who? If Jesus did not actually rise from the dead, there are basically three options: the Romans, the Jewish leaders, or the Christians. Is it possible that one of these groups could have taken the body of Jesus?

The Romans Stole the Body

What possible reason would the Romans have had to steal Jesus' body? They had nothing to gain from an empty tomb. What they wanted more than anything was tranquility and peace. An empty tomb would only cause chaos and confusion, first in Judea and then throughout the Empire. Even if, for some inexplicable reason, the Romans *had* stolen the body and the Christians had begun to make a fuss about the resurrection, the Romans could have simply brought forth the body of Jesus and put an end to the unrest between Jewish leaders and the young Christian Church.

In fact, the Roman procurator, Pontius Pilate, actually provided a team of armed soldiers to secure the tomb, precisely *because* the Jewish leaders were concerned that the apostles might try to steal the body. Roman discipline was harsh. If a Roman soldier fell asleep on the job, he was potentially subject to execution. Thus, Roman soldiers were highly motivated to stay awake and alert while on watch. To lose the body of a controversial person whom they put to death would have brought about severe consequences. There is simply no reason to think that the Romans would have stolen the body of Jesus.

The Jewish Leaders Stole the Body

As with the Romans, the Jewish leaders had nothing to gain and everything to lose by stealing the body of Jesus from the tomb. They themselves made clear that they were concerned by Jesus' promises of a resurrection.

> The next day, that is, after the Day of Preparation, the chief priests and the Pharisees gathered before Pilate and said, "Sir, we remember how that impostor said, while he was still alive, 'After three days I will rise again.' Therefore, order the tomb to be made secure until the third day, lest his disciples go and steal him away and tell the people 'He has risen from the dead.'" Pilate said to them, "You have a guard of soldiers; go, make it as secure as

you can." So, they went and made the tomb secure.
(Mt 27:62-66)

The Jewish leaders went through a great deal of trouble to
have Jesus crucified. They wanted him dead and certainly did
not want him coming back from the dead. So they, too, had
nothing to gain with an empty tomb—and if they had stolen
the body for some unimaginable reason, they certainly would
have produced it as soon as the Christians began claiming that
Jesus had risen from the dead. Yet their only explanation for
the empty tomb was that the apostles had stolen the body. Also,
a Roman or Jewish theft of Jesus' body does not explain the
multiple reports of encounters with the risen Christ, ranging
from Mary Magdalene, to the disciples on the Emmaus Road,
to the apostles on several occasions, to more than five hundred
people at once.

The Apostles Stole the Body

So far, we have looked at every common (if not crazy)
alternative explanation except for the one actually offered in the
Bible. In Matthew 28:11-15, we read that the Jewish leaders told
the Roman guards to say that Jesus' disciples had come by night
and stolen him away. The Jewish leaders even offered to cover
for the Roman guards with their superiors.

But is this really plausible? A typical Roman guard
contingent consisted of sixteen or more soldiers. In this scenario,

it would be necessary for all of these guards to have fallen asleep, even though they faced execution for doing so. The alternative is that the apostles, by stealth, were able to sneak up on these sixteen trained guards, roll the stone away, and make off with Jesus' body—even though these same apostles had been cowering in fear the day before. If they had lacked the courage to defend Jesus while he was alive, where would they now find the courage to steal his body?

The bottom line is this: If the apostles had stolen the body of Jesus and then falsely claimed that he had risen, not only would they have been liars; they would have been the most amazing group of liars in the history of the world. For the rest of their lives, not a single one of these men ever renounced the resurrection. Even more incredibly, all of the apostles except John were killed for preaching the Gospel. They all paid in blood for their faith in the risen Christ.

In fact, they paid in blood many times because they didn't just *die* as martyrs. They *lived* as martyrs as well, enduring persecution, exile, scourging, punishment, abuse, and imprisonment far from their homes and far from one another. The psychology of this is important to note. As a group, they held to their faith in the resurrection, but they didn't all suffer death in a group. It might be conceivable that a group of eleven men, in the grip of momentary religious hysteria, could convince one another to die together. But, they didn't do that. These eleven men were killed over a period of forty years, hundreds of miles apart from one another, and not a single one ever renounced the claim that Jesus had actually risen from the dead. In fact, they themselves made it clear that more than five hundred people had seen the risen Christ, and they convinced thousands more who had never met Jesus to accept death for their belief in the resurrection. Not a single one of them gained any earthly profit for his belief. What possible motive would they have had for saying Jesus had risen from the dead if they knew he had not? In short, it is totally implausible that the apostles could have stolen Jesus' body.

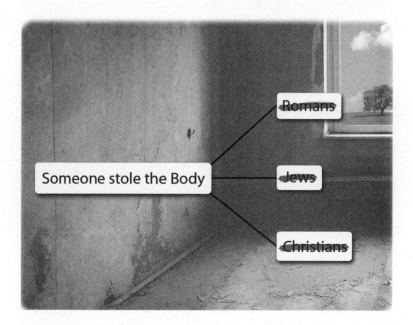

There are no other options. Jesus' body is gone and there is no explanation—except the one offered by the apostles: "The Lord has risen indeed" (Lk 24:34). And because he is alive, he stands before each one of us and calls us to answer that same question he put to his apostles, the most important question ever asked in the history of the world:

Who Do You Say That I Am?

If none of the alternative explanations about the identity and resurrection of Jesus works, then the only other option is to acknowledge that Jesus' claims are true: he is God and he has been raised from the dead for the salvation of the world. And this leaves us with a profoundly important choice. We can choose to accept him or reject him. This is our free choice; no one can make it for us. We can choose to reject Jesus, or we can fall on our knees before him as St. Thomas did and cry out, "My Lord and my God!"

If we choose to accept Christ, we choose to follow him as the Lord of our life. Since Jesus is a King, he must have a kingdom. We will look at what this means in the next chapter.

CHAPTER 4

THE KINGDOM OF GOD ON EARTH

Jesus gave his life to take away the sins of the world and reconcile everyone to God the Father. But the question remains, "How do we come in contact with the power and truth of Christ today, some 2,000 years after the event?" The answer is that Jesus established his Kingdom here on earth: the Kingdom of God. That is what following Jesus means: Christians accept Jesus as the King of the Universe and King of our lives. When we do that, we reject the "kingdoms of this world" in favor of the Kingdom of God by obeying Jesus as Lord of our lives. So how do we allow the Lordship of Jesus to extend into every aspect of our lives? What are we supposed to believe? How are we supposed to act? The Scriptures tell us: "Trust in the Lord with all your heart, and do not rely on your own insight. In all your ways acknowledge him, and he will make straight your paths" (Prv 3:5-6).

In other words, God desires to change the way we think—about everything. But how can we know what God is asking of us? Yes, he gave us the Bible, and we ought to form the way we think according to what it teaches. But there are many different interpretations of the Bible. Thousands of groups claim that their beliefs are based upon the Bible, and yet they often contradict one another. The question is not "what does the Bible *say*?" but "what does the Bible *mean*?"

Finding the Right Path

Fortunately, Jesus founded a Church to lead all people to unity with God and one another. In Chapter 2, when we considered the question of whether we can trust the Bible, we turned to history for the answer. We discovered that the writings of the early Christians bear witness to the content of the biblical texts; their quotations from the Scriptures are irrefutable evidence that these texts have not been distorted over the centuries.

These same believers also bear witness to the *meaning* of the Bible. The early Christians did not simply quote the sacred texts; they shared a common understanding of these texts and commented upon them. When we turn to the early Church Fathers (i.e., Christian leaders and scholars of the earliest centuries), there is wide agreement not only about what the Bible said, but also about what the Bible meant. So when a question arises about a specific passage, we can turn to these important witnesses. By themselves, the Church Fathers do not have the authority that Scripture does—but where there is broad or even unanimous agreement on a particular issue of biblical interpretation, we can be confident that we have found the correct meaning of a sacred passage.

Remember, the Fathers of the Church were in a unique

position: They had been taught by the apostles or by companions of the apostles; they shared a cultural and a linguistic heritage that was much closer to the apostles than is ours today; and they lived at a time when being a Christian meant suffering for your beliefs. Therefore, when these earliest witnesses have a unanimous perspective on a particular biblical text, this is compelling evidence that their interpretation reflects the real teaching of Jesus and his apostles. With this in mind, let's look again at who Jesus is and what he came to do.

The King Has a Kingdom

Asking Jesus to be the Lord of your life changes everything; every aspect of your life is now defined by your complete loyalty to him. Indeed the entire world can be divided into those who live their lives in loyalty to Christ and those who don't. Think about it: The very God who created the universe and governs the cosmos has come to you to seek your personal loyalty. Jesus is not merely asking us to acknowledge that he exists or that he did good deeds a long time ago in a far-away land. He is telling us he is alive and present *now* and that he wants to enter into relationship with us. Being in relationship with him is the key to everything. As we begin to live in his Lordship, we come to realize just how far things in the world have gone wrong.

Originally, humanity was placed here by a loving Father. We were intended to live in unity with God and each other, but the world has undergone a revolt—and the consequences have been devastating. What was intended to be our home has become a battlefield. Not only has the world forgotten our Creator, each of us has participated in this revolt. Think of the many times we have chosen to ignore—or even reject—the ways of God. Each of us bears the wounds of this rebellion: wars, famine, disease, injustice, and hatred are all consequences of this war. Sin makes us slaves to our passions, and we find ourselves seeking the pleasures of this world without any sense that we have been made for something more—for greatness and everlasting joy. We are drawn back to our senses when we hear Jesus' call, "Repent, for the kingdom of heaven is at hand" (Mt 4:17).

It is notable that Jesus' entire life was ordered around the proclamation of this kingdom. He began his ministry proclaiming it and spent his days preaching about what his kingdom was like (see Mt 13:31, 13:44, 13:47, 20:1). He went to his death crucified as "the king of the Jews" (Jn 19:19), and since his resurrection and ascension he has been recognized as the "King of kings" (Rv 19:16).

The fact that Jesus is a king is not news in heaven, where the angels give him glory continuously. The noteworthy aspect of the "good news" (which is what *gospel* means) is that Jesus came to earth to establish an "outpost" of his kingdom *here* in the midst of the rebellion. Anyone who desires to join him can switch his allegiance from a world that is passing away to the Kingdom that will never end.

The groundwork for the coming of God's kingdom had been

laid many years before when God liberated his chosen people Israel from slavery in Egypt, brought them to the Promised Land, and made them into a kingdom. At this time, about a thousand years before the birth of Jesus, God established David in Jerusalem as king over his people. In David's kingdom we see the blueprints for the everlasting kingdom God would bring about through the long-foretold figure of the "Son of David"—Jesus.

Jesus Christ, the Son of David

Jesus was not, of course, born in an historical vacuum. He comes from a people with a long and rich heritage—a great people who, by the time of Jesus, had fallen on hard times. The Jews looked back with longing to a "golden age" and looked forward with hope to the rise of a great king and his restored kingdom.

This golden age was a thousand years earlier, when King David took the throne. Those were the good times, when God had established David to guide Israel and the other nations of the world. God also swore to David that he would "establish the throne of his kingdom forever" (2 Sm 7:13-16). Unfortunately, the good times didn't last, and over the centuries Israel was beaten, deported, returned, trampled upon, and finally occupied by the Romans. But through it all, the Jewish people clung to the promise given by God to David: that one day, one of David's descendants would arise and establish an everlasting kingdom.

The "Son of David" has different titles in the writings of

the prophets who lived in the centuries before Jesus, but the most famous one is *Messiah* (or *Christos* in Greek), which means "anointed one" (see Is 61:1). When Jesus answers to the title "Son of David" (as he does throughout the gospels), he was accepting the title of the Messianic King, the Christ. Likewise, when he rides a donkey into Jerusalem on the Sunday before his crucifixion, he is making the same claim, because that is exactly what King Solomon, the very first "son of David," had done when he entered on his reign (1 Kgs 1:38-40). The Jewish people knew this and greeted him with shouts of "hosanna to the Son of David."

So what does the kingdom of the Son of David—the Kingdom of God—look like? To get some clues, we should remember what the risen Christ himself did while walking on the Emmaus Road with two of his followers: "And beginning with Moses and all the prophets, he interpreted to them in all the Scriptures the things concerning himself" (Lk 24:27).

Jesus told his disciples that he was fulfilling what God had spoken throughout the Old Testament:

> Then he opened their minds to understand the
> Scriptures, and said to them, "Thus it is written,
> that the Christ should suffer and on the third day
> rise from the dead, and that repentance and forgive-
> ness of sins should be preached in his name to all

nations, beginning from Jerusalem. You are witnesses of these things. (Lk 24:45-48)

In short, Jesus invited his hearers to think back over the
history of Israel—including the kingdom of David—so that they
would understand his Kingdom. In other words, he is saying
that when we say "yes" to him and acknowledge that he is God
the Son in human flesh, risen from the dead, this will involve
more than just a personal and private conversion; it will involve
uniting ourselves with all the other people who acknowledge
him as king. In reality, if we accept Jesus as king, we must also
accept his Kingdom. We cannot embrace the king while refusing
to embrace his Kingdom.

So where is this kingdom today? How can we recognize and
enter into this kingdom? Before we can answer these questions
about Jesus' Kingdom, we need to examine some of the essential
aspects of David's kingdom. Let's take a look at three fundamental
institutions which shaped the royal dynasty: the king, the prime
minister, and the queen mother.

The King

David was a great and powerful king, but what made David's
kingdom so amazing was God's extraordinary promise that one
of his descendants would arise and be even greater than he was.

I will raise up your offspring after you, who shall
come forth from your body, and I will establish his

> kingdom. He shall build a house for my name, and
> I will establish the throne of his kingdom forever.
> I will be his father, and he shall be my son. (2 Sm
> 7:12-14)

During times of difficulty, Israel held on to the hope that God would eventually fulfill his promise and send a great king—the Messiah—to save them from their enemies. He would bring God's truth to the Israelites and to all of the nations, and his kingdom would last forever.

> For to us a child is born, to us a son is given; and
> the government will be upon his shoulder, and his
> name will be called "Wonderful Counselor, Mighty
> God, Everlasting Father, Prince of Peace." Of the
> increase of his government and of peace there will
> be no end, upon the throne of David, and over his
> kingdom, to establish it, and to uphold it with jus-
> tice and with righteousness from this time forth and
> for evermore. (Is 9:6-7)

Unlike any other kingdom in the history of the world, the kingdom promised to David would extend not just to the borders of Israel, but to the ends of the earth and to the end of time.

When David became king, he could have ruled from any city but chose Jerusalem. Why? The answer can be seen in David's actions. When he entered upon his reign, he did two crucial things. First, he retrieved the Ark of the Covenant, the golden box that contained the fragments of the Ten Commandments given by God to Moses on Mount Sinai, from a shrine miles to the north and brought it to Jerusalem. As the great sign of the Mosaic covenant, it was the holiest object in all of Israel. As the Ark came down the road, David danced before it in a special robe called an *ephod*. As part of the renewal of the covenant with God, he offered the people gifts of bread and wine (2 Sm 6).

What is unique here is that David the king was dressing and acting like a priest. That is the meaning of the ephod and the offerings of bread and wine. In fact, he was acting like another priest-king who had ruled Jerusalem long before: Melchizedek, who had offered the same gifts of bread and wine when David's ancient ancestor Abraham returned from a great battle (Gn 14:17-20). King David saw himself as a priest-king, offering bread and wine just as Melchizedek had. Like Melchizedek, his reign combined the royal palace of the king with the sacred temple of the priest in a new way.

The Prime Minister

Since antiquity, kings have often had prime ministers to govern temporal affairs, and David was no exception. The prime minister, or *al-bayit* ("head of the household"), was a man placed second to the king who would possess the king's authority. We see this, for instance, in Isaiah 22, when God grants this office to a man named Eliakim:

> In that day I will call my servant Eliakim the son of
> Hilkiah, and I will clothe him with your robe, and
> will bind your belt on him, and will commit your
> authority to his hand; and he shall be a father to the
> inhabitants of Jerusalem and to the house of Judah.
> And I will place on his shoulder the key of the house
> of David; he shall open, and none shall shut; and he
> shall shut, and none shall open. And I will fasten
> him like a peg in a sure place, and he will become a
> throne of honor to his father's house (Is 22:20-23).

As king of God's chosen people, David was a father to the
people he governed. Now, his fatherly role is shared with the *al-bayit*. Once he became prime minister, Eliakim had a fatherly role as
well. And with that fatherly role comes both authority (symbolized
by the keys) and honor (symbolized by the throne).

The Queen Mother

Another vital office in the Davidic kingdom was that of the
queen mother. We are told in Scripture that each of the Davidic
kings had a queen. What is unusual about the queen from our
modern perspective is that the queen was never the *wife* of the
king, but was always his *mother*. Each royal mother, or *gebirah*,
reigned with her son and had a primary role of bringing petitions
before the king so that he could rule. Consider the following
scene from Solomon's reign:

So Bathsheba went to King Solomon, to speak to
him on behalf of Adonijah. And the king rose to
meet her, and bowed down to her; then he sat on
his throne, and had a seat brought for the king's
mother; and she sat on his right. (1 Kgs 2:19)

The office of the queen mother is exemplified in this passage.
The queen mother comes to her son, the king, in order to speak
on behalf of another. The king honors his mother by rising to his
feet as she enters the room and bowing before her. Even though
he is king, she is still his mother and he is bound by the fourth
commandment: Honor your father and mother. This honor
shown the queen mother is extraordinary, as the king would not
bow to anyone else. Even his wives were required to bow before
him (1 Kgs 1:16). The queen mother uses her position of honor
to intercede for others. All members of the kingdom can bring
their concerns before the king, but when his mother intercedes
on their behalf, their petitions are elevated before him.

The King and His Kingdom

With this little overview of the kingdom of David in mind,
let us now return to Jesus and his proclamation of the kingdom
of God. The first verse of the New Testament (Matthew 1:1)
introduces Jesus as the son of David and, as we have seen,
the Davidic kingdom established structures that Jesus and his
followers would have understood and taken for granted. So it is

only natural that when the Son of David—Jesus—establishes his kingdom by his death and resurrection, we see his queen mother and prime minister also taking their places around him.

For instance, we notice that in Matthew's gospel, Jesus seems to conceal his identity for much of his public life. Only after Peter openly acknowledges him as the Christ (Mt 16:16) does Jesus begin to declare openly his identity as the Son of David and bestow on Peter the "keys of the kingdom," a symbolic gesture by which Jesus establishes Peter as prime minister of this new and everlasting kingdom. It is not a coincidence that "keys" are also mentioned in the reference to the prime minister Eliakim in Isaiah 22. The Church Fathers saw this pattern and said as much. Jesus, the Messianic Son of David, was building his kingdom on the model of his father David, and it, too, would have a prime minister who could act with the authority delegated him by the Christ.

Similarly, any Israelite would have understood the implications when Mary, who is pregnant with Jesus, is greeted by her kinswoman Elizabeth in Luke 1:39-56. Elizabeth exclaims, "[How is it] that the mother of my Lord should come to me?" This phrase "mother of my Lord" is the ancient greeting for the queen mother. By acknowledging Mary as queen, Elizabeth is, at the same time, declaring the unborn babe in Mary's womb to be the Messiah. Honor given to the queen mother is always honor also given to her son, the king.

What All this Means to You

There is one more feature in the Kingdom of God we cannot overlook: you. The Kingdom is no ordinary kingdom, and you are no ordinary subject. You are royalty. This is the kingdom of the New Covenant. But what exactly is a "covenant," anyway?

A covenant is a sacred bond of relationship. From biblical times to the present, covenants have been used to form families. Two classic forms of covenants are adoption and marriage. So profound is the change brought about by a covenant that it is very much akin to the difference between slavery and sonship, or prostitution and marriage. In slavery and prostitution, people *use* one another for a selfish end. In sonship and marriage, people *belong* to one another in a life-giving union.

Covenant relationships are rich and multi-dimensional. Consider my relationship with my wife. We are more than good friends; we are family. We share a bond of sacred kinship. She is not just my girlfriend; she is my wife. And because our relationship is a covenant, it doesn't stop there: her mother and father have become *my* mother and father. Her sisters have become *my* sisters. Because of the covenantal nature of a relationship, it is not just my wife and me but all of us. My children have two sets of grandparents, and my wife's parents are just as much my children's grandparents as my own parents are. Our covenant has made a family out of people who had not been family. Similarly, the New Covenant does not just unite us to God; it reunites us with one another.

So if a covenant forms family bonds, how are covenants made? Throughout history, covenants have been formed through sacred ritual and liturgy. There are essentially two parts:

1. A *sacred oath*, which calls upon God to hold each party to faithfulness and to assist them in their new relationship. In marriage, this is the sworn promise to be faithful and open to life, "so help me God."

2. A *ritual act* that manifests the nature of the oaths. In baptism, this is the pouring of, or immersion into, water which symbolizes both death and rebirth; this brings about rebirth and adoption as sons and daughters of God.

Covenant rituals are as old as recorded human history, but what is unique about the Judeo-Christian tradition is that God is not merely called upon to *witness* the covenant; he is a *participant*. The Hebrew word for "oath" (*shevua*) is root for the word meaning "seven" (*sheva*). The New Covenant is founded upon seven sacred oath rituals by which Jesus the King shares his very life with his followers. In Latin, the word for "oath" is *sacramentum*. The New Covenant is founded upon seven oaths, or sacraments. God is calling each of us to something far more than a political alliance. He is calling us into covenantal relationship. The way that each of us enters into the kingdom is by adoption—through the rebirth of baptism. Each of us is called to be a son or daughter of the King. Jesus has chosen to impart his life through the sacraments of the New Covenant. Because of these oaths and liturgical rituals, we are not merely subjects; we have become family.

This has amazing implications. It means God is not just our King but our Father. We aren't just governed by him; we are loved by him. In fact, relationship is the very essence of the kingdom. Just as we have a personal relationship with Jesus the King, we are called to a personal loyalty to his prime minister. This office, given to Peter and his successors, allows the prime minister to act on behalf of the King. Therefore, the prime minister manifests a fatherly role as well. This is exactly what the Scriptures tell us when we read of the prime minister that "he shall be a father to the inhabitants of Jerusalem" (Is 22:21). That is also why the successor of St. Peter, the prime minster, is called the "pope" (from "papa"). The pope is father to all of Christ's earthly followers on earth. Our common loyalty to him is a *family trait* that serves to preserve unity in the Church, which is the kingdom of God on earth.

The relationships don't stop there. If we are adopted children of God, then Jesus has given us *his* Father as *our* Father. And, if his Father is our Father, then his mother must also be our mother. This is precisely what Jesus tells his beloved disciple when, from the cross, he declares to him, "Behold, your mother," and says to Mary, "Behold, your son!" (Jn 19:26-27). The queen mother is also our mother, because we have become adopted sons and daughters of the Father. She lives to exercise her maternal and royal care for us before the King.

Think about this. We are not merely "saved" orphans; we have been restored as full members of the family—indeed, as members of the royal family itself! If we have God for our Father, then we each have Mary as our mother, and, just like the King, we are called to honor her by the commandment to honor our mother. This honor is profound, but is completely different from the adoration that is given to the Blessed Trinity alone. We adore Christ, who is God made man, and we imitate him in honoring his mother.

So the gospels are the story of Jesus and those around him consciously establishing the universal kingdom of the Son of David, and it is for this kingdom that he will be crucified. But this death is not the last word for this Son of David. As we shall see, after he rises from the dead, his kingdom begins to spread throughout the world, transforming not merely nations, kingdoms, civilizations, and cultures, but each of us from the inside by the power of his sacraments, through the working of the Holy Spirit.

CHAPTER 5

LIFE IN THE KINGDOM

Jesus came to seek and save the lost by establishing the Kingdom of God. The manner in which Jesus goes about building his kingdom might catch us by surprise. Throughout the gospels, people continually discover his royal dignity: Elizabeth and the unborn John the Baptist identify the Son of David before he is even born (Lk 1:41-44). The prophets Simeon and Anna recognize the Messiah King when he is only a few days old (Lk 2:25-38), and the Magi come from the East to honor the child born a king (Mt 2:1-12). Once Jesus begins his teaching and healing, the people recognize him as the Son of David. Even the demons acknowledge him as the Messiah (Mk 1:23-26). What is odd is not that people recognize Jesus for who he is, but that he responds as he docs.

The long-awaited Son of David seems almost reluctant to actually allow himself to be made a king. He spends much of his public ministry in out-of-the-way villages, only coming to Jerusalem—the city of the king—for religious celebrations and then quickly leaving again. He works miracles, but he frequently tells those he has healed to tell no one how it happened. Why work miracles, attract the attention of people looking for you, and then avoid and even flee the very people who would crown you as King? Because Jesus knows that their faith in him, while real, is still just the beginning. Accepting the King and his Kingdom will require a faith empowered from on high. Following Jesus requires more than obedience or faith. He must transform us from the inside out.

We have already seen how the structure of this new and everlasting Kingdom resembles the kingdom of David. Jesus certainly has David's kingdom in mind, but he has come to bring much more. While God has given us glimpses of what he has prepared for us, what he actually desires to bring is beyond our wildest imaginings and hopes. We will miss the Kingdom altogether if we limit God to what we imagine or expect, as the prophets proclaimed long ago: "For my thoughts are not your thoughts, neither are your ways my ways, says the LORD" (Is 55:8).

The external structures of the Kingdom—the king, the prime minister, and the queen mother—are intended to support a profound transformation that must take place within each of us—a complete change that will be mystical, liturgical, and incarnational. Jesus will institute sacred oaths and ritual acts that communicate divine power to us by means that both symbolize what they do and do what they symbolize. In other words, the Kingdom will be *sacramental*.

To see this more clearly, let's look at the gospel of John. Here we see that the public ministry of Jesus takes place in a way that is carefully linked to the liturgical feasts and holy days of the Jewish liturgical calendar. Judaism is a liturgical faith that marks the passing of time with various religious celebrations. Jesus used the rhythm of these sacred events over the course of his three-year ministry to highlight his intentions for the Kingdom.

Three Passovers

Of all the Jewish celebrations, the most central was the Passover. Each Passover served to recall the events of the past and anticipate future blessings. At Passover, the Jewish people were reminded of their own identity as God's chosen people. Faithful Jews would make a pilgrimage to Jerusalem for the great feast. *The Poem of the Four Nights* is an ancient Jewish writing that was used in the liturgy of the synagogue.[5] According to this poem, Passover celebrated four great events, three of which had already occurred by Jesus' time.

The first three great events that were celebrated during the Passover were the creation of the universe, the calling of the patriarch Abraham, and the Exodus led by Moses. The fourth, still awaited at the time of Jesus, was the coming of the Messiah who would bring about redemption. Each Passover, then, served

---

[5] Targum Neophyti. See *Neophyti I, vol 2.* (Madrid-Barcelona, 1970) 312-13, as cited in Lucien Deiss, *It's the Lord's Supper* (London: Collins, 1975), 35

to remind the chosen people of God's care for them in the past and to heighten their expectation for the coming Messiah.

During the three years of his public ministry, Jesus carefully prepares his followers to receive his Kingdom. If we follow Jesus through the three Passover celebrations that take place during his public ministry, we see him establish the New and Everlasting Covenant, which will bring about the Kingdom of God. Everything that Jesus says and does leads his followers to trust him more deeply. Such trust is absolutely essential because what Jesus has come to bring is so much more than anyone could have imagined. Jesus shows us the essential nature of the sacraments—how they will take our faith and transform it into something more, something supernatural.

The Beginning of the Kingdom – Baptism

John's gospel begins with the baptism of Jesus. Following his baptism, Jesus performs his first wonder—the changing of water into wine at the wedding feast of Cana. The other gospels typically describe the mighty works of Jesus as miracles, and so they are. But John highlights the fact that these miracles are not just amazing works but "signs" intended to point us to the deeper reality they signify. If we see the wonder, but miss the *sign*, we will entirely miss the point. We will be like someone who stares at the tip of a pointed finger instead of looking at what the finger is pointing to.

At each of the three Passovers during his public ministry,

Jesus highlights the sacred and divine aspects of the Kingdom. In John's gospel, the first of these Passovers takes place after his first sign at the wedding feast at Cana, when Jesus goes to Jerusalem. During this first Passover, Jesus reveals the first of the sacraments he intends for his followers: baptism.

Jesus, the King, enters his royal city, cleanses the Temple of the money changers, and declares, "Destroy this temple, and in three days I will raise it up" (Jn 2:19). The bold actions and miraculous signs he performs lead people to believe in him. But his response to this new popularity will show us that he is looking for more than mere human faith or recognition. He is calling his followers to a covenant—a sacred family bond—not merely friendship. Let's see what happens when one of the Jewish leaders comes to Jesus:

> Now when he was in Jerusalem at the Passover feast, many *believed* in his name when they saw the signs which he did; but Jesus did not *trust* himself to them, because he knew *all men* and needed no one to bear witness of *man*; for he himself knew what was in *man*.

> Now there was a man of the Pharisees, named Nicodemus, a ruler of the Jews. This man came to Jesus by night and said to him, "Rabbi, we know that you are a teacher come from God; for no one

> can do these signs that you do, unless God is with
> him. (Jn 2:23–3:2, emphasis added)

Something odd is going on here. People believed in Jesus, which would appear to be just what he wanted. Isn't that why he came? Isn't that why he worked his signs? But Jesus did not *trust* himself to them. The Greek word for *believe* and *trust* is actually the same word (*pisteuo*). People believed in Jesus, but he did not believe in them. In other words, faith is necessary, but faith alone will not suffice; something more is needed.

This is quite a moment. Jesus has come to the city of the king on the great feast of Passover. Jerusalem would have been filled with God's chosen people, who were longing for the coming of the Messiah. In this context, Jesus works miracles and cleanses the Temple, and many believe in him. Among these early believers is Nicodemus, a ruler of the Jews. It would appear that Jesus' acceptance by an important member of the ruling class should certainly be a foundational moment for the Kingdom.

Jesus, though, is waiting for something more. He tells Nicodemus: "Truly, truly, I say to you, unless one is born anew, he cannot see the kingdom of God" (Jn 3:3).

Entering God's Kingdom takes faith—but more than just faith. To enter the Kingdom, we must be spiritually reborn.

Jesus continues, "Truly, truly, I say to you, unless one is born of water and the Spirit, he cannot enter the kingdom of God" (Jn 3:5).

Jesus does not reject the faith of Nicodemus but calls him to something more—to the rebirth of baptism. To see more clearly what Jesus means, we can look to the context of this passage within Scripture and the witness of history.

Scripture always needs to be read in context. Jesus says that we must be "born of water and the spirit." Are there any other references to "water" and "spirit" in John's gospel? We are told that Jesus is baptized in the water of the Jordan, and the spirit descended upon him (Jn 1:26-32, as well as Mt 3:16; Mk 1:9-11; Lk 3:21-22). Immediately after this interaction with Nicodemus, we are told that Jesus and his disciples were baptizing others.[6] The context therefore indicates that Jesus is speaking about baptism. If we want to come into the kingdom, we must become children of God; we must be adopted into the royal family of the great king. Baptism is the covenantal act by which we are reborn as adopted sons and daughters of God.

This is precisely what the witness of history shows us. For instance, St. Peter tells us that baptism forgives sins: "And Peter said to them, 'Repent, and be baptized every one of you in the name of Jesus Christ for the forgiveness of your sins; and you shall receive the gift of the holy spirit'" (Acts 2:38).

---

[6] Some might question the connection of baptism and the Holy Spirit, citing John 7:39, which states that "as yet the Spirit had not been given, because Jesus was not yet glorified." But this statement actually affirms that the Spirit would be given after the resurrection. Each of the sacraments of the New Covenant derives its power from the death and resurrection of Jesus.

St. Paul tells us that we are saved and regenerated (that is, *reborn*) in baptism:

> [W]hen the goodness and loving kindness of God our Savior appeared, he saved us, not because of deeds done by us in righteousness, but in virtue of his own mercy, by the washing of regeneration and renewal in the Holy Spirit, which he poured out upon us richly through Jesus Christ our Savior, so that we might be justified by his grace and become heirs in hope of eternal life (Ti 3:4-7).

The Church's teaching on the necessity of baptism has remained constant throughout history. In the second century, the Christian apologist Tertullian wrote:

> Since it is in fact prescribed that no one can attain to salvation without baptism, especially in view of that declaration of the Lord, who says: "Unless a man shall be born of water, he shall not have life.[7]

And in the third century the Christian philosopher Origen added:

---

[7]Tertullian, *On Baptism*, ch. 12. Trans., Rev. S. Thelwall. http://www.newadvent.org/fathers/0321.

> The church received from the apostles the tradition
> of giving Baptism even to infants. For the apostles,
> to whom were committed the secrets of divine
> mysteries, knew that there is in everyone the innate
> stains of sin, which must be washed away through
> water and the Spirit.[8]

This marks a revelation of the first of the sacraments that will be established in the New Covenant. But Jesus has even more in mind.

The Heart of the Kingdom – The Eucharist

A year passes, and we see the second Passover of Jesus' public ministry. Just as Jesus gave a great sign the year before by changing water into wine (Jn 2:1-12), this year, as he is teaching the crowds, he manifests his power through another great sign (Jn 6:1-15). He takes a few loaves of bread and a couple of fish and feeds more than five thousand men (not counting women and children). As the crowd following Jesus notes, the miracle of bread reminds them of when God fed the people of Israel in Moses' time with bread from heaven (Jn 6:30-31; also see Ex 16).

From a merely natural perspective this would be the perfect moment for Jesus to declare himself. The Son of David has come to build his kingdom and his people want to make him king.

The crowd is ready to make Jesus king on their terms.

---

[8]Origen, *Commentary on the Epistle to the Romans*

However, the people following after Jesus see the wonder but not the sign. He wants to feed their starving souls, but they only see the earthly bread. They prepare to take Jesus and make him king, hoping for a ruler who will provide them with an unending supply of food. And again, from a merely natural perspective, it would appear that, surely, now is the time for him to declare himself. Jesus, the Son of David, is being pursued by his people. He has come to build his Kingdom, and they want to make him king. It would appear to be the perfect opportunity. Yet what does Jesus do? He flees!

A year before, we saw a Jewish leader, Nicodemus, seeking entrance into the Kingdom, but Jesus told him that more than human faith is necessary: he must be reborn in baptism. Now, a year later, the crowds are ready to make Jesus king, and again he shows them that their human faith and desire are good but something more is waiting for them. That something is, again, both covenantal and mystical: he calls us to the sacrament of the Eucharist. Once the crowds calm down, Jesus returns and tells them:

> "I am the bread of life. Your fathers ate the manna in the wilderness, and they died. This is the bread which comes down from heaven, that a man may eat of it and not die. I am the living bread which came down from heaven; if any one eats of this

bread, he will live for ever; and the bread which I shall give for the life of the world is my flesh." The Jews then disputed among themselves, saying "How can this man give us his flesh to eat?" So Jesus said to them, "Truly, truly, I say to you, unless you eat the flesh of the Son of man and drink his blood, you have no life in you; he who eats my flesh and drinks my blood has eternal life, and I will raise him up at the last day. For my flesh is food indeed, and my blood is drink indeed. He who eats my flesh and drinks my blood abides in me, and I in him. As the living Father sent me, and I live because of the Father, so he who eats me will live because of me." (Jn 6:48–57)

A year earlier, Nicodemus had come with faith but without understanding. Now the crowds who wanted to force Jesus to become an earthly king are likewise confused and even scandalized. They react: "This is a hard saying; who can listen to it?" (Jn 6:60).

Indeed, people begin to leave. But rather than running after them and explaining that his words were meant to be taken only figuratively, Jesus lets them leave. He then turns and asks his apostles: "Will you also go away?" (Jn 6:67).

Peter responds with more than mere human faith. He does not know how to interpret the Lord's words, but he has come to trust him completely. He simply answers: "Lord, to whom shall we go? You have the words of eternal life; and we have believed, and come to know that you are the Holy One of God" (Jn 6:68–69).

Peter has come to understand the deeper reality to which the signs point: Jesus is the Holy One of God. He is willing to trust Jesus even though he does not yet understand what he is telling them. Peter and the other apostles are following their king as he prepares to manifest his Kingdom.

How is Peter able to do what Nicodemus and the five-thousand cannot yet do? Only by trusting in Jesus and accepting God's help. In doing so, Peter becomes more himself, not less.

> Believing is possible only by grace and the interior helps of the Holy Spirit. But it is no less true that believing is an authentically human act. Trusting in God and cleaving to the truths he has revealed are contrary neither to human freedom nor to human reason. (*CCC* 154)

Still, Peter, along with the other apostles, will need to wait another year—until Jesus' next and final Passover—before the meaning of Christ's mysterious words concerning his body and blood will become crystal clear.

The Mercy of the Kingdom – Confession

The third and final Passover finds Jesus again back in Jerusalem. Once again Jesus is recognized as King, and this time by a multitude. As he rides on a donkey into the Holy City, they cry out: "Hosanna to the Son of David! Blessed is he who comes in the name of the Lord! Hosanna in the highest!" (Mt 21:9).

The wisdom of Jesus is becoming clear. Each previous time the people showed faith in him, he would withdraw and point them to something deeper—and each time the crowds grew, as did their zeal for the Kingdom. Surely, now is the time. Surely now Jesus will accept their pleas and take his throne. And that is precisely what he does. But the way in which Jesus takes possession of his kingdom is altogether unexpected and amazing.

He goes to the rulers of the day and condemns them for their hypocrisy. He goes to the Temple and predicts its complete destruction, a prophecy that will be fulfilled in A.D. 70, less than a generation later. His words and actions ultimately drive the Jewish leaders to demand his life, and the mob turns against him. Jesus seems on the verge of establishing his kingdom, yet he again acts against what would seem to be the prudent and logical course. A modern-day public relations expert would have counseled against his statements to the Jewish leaders, but Jesus' mind is not dominated by the world's fascination with "image." As a result of his actions, he will soon watch as the multitudes, who just a few days before had hailed him as king, cry out, "Crucify him! Crucify him!" (Mk 15:13-14).

But before the indignant leaders and angry crowd can have their way with him, Jesus will share one final meal with his apostles. This third and final Passover meal is the Last Supper.

Jesus is alone with his chosen men. Outside, the leaders are ready to kill him, and one of his own—Judas—has just left the meal to go and betray Jesus. As soon as Judas departs, Jesus says, "Now is the Son of man glorified, and in him God is glorified" (Jn 13:31).

Now is the time? It *wasn't* time when Nicodemus came to him to express his faith? It *wasn't* time when the crowds came to make him king by force after he fed the thousands? It *wasn't* time, just a few days earlier, when the multitudes welcomed him into Jerusalem?

No. But now *is* the time, just as he prepares to lay his life down for the sake of his Bride, the Church. Jesus knew that, for us to experience all of what he has in store for us, he must first lay down his life. Through his death and resurrection, the sacraments of the New Covenant will receive their power. When he goes back to his Father, they (the Father and the Son) will send the Holy Spirit, and the apostles will be sent into the world. Jesus reveals this truth when he says: "Unless a grain of wheat falls into the earth and dies, it remains by itself alone; but if it dies, it bears much fruit" (Jn 12:24).

This final Passover for Jesus will include his Last Supper, death, resurrection, and the commissioning of his apostles on

Easter Sunday. In the midst of this drama, the apostles will be scattered, and Peter will even deny his Lord three times.

Arrested, tried, tortured, and crucified, Jesus returns to his Father. But, just as he promised, this was not the end of the story. On Sunday morning, the tomb is empty, and some of the women who had accompanied the disciples report that they have seen Jesus risen from the dead. The apostles are in a state of shock, huddled together and fearing for their lives. On Easter Sunday evening, the risen Jesus appears in their midst. It is hard to imagine the range of emotions they must have felt. Jesus, whom they loved, is risen from the dead! This is great news! And at the same time, they must have been pierced with the realization that they had abandoned him in his hour of need. What would he say? They haven't long to find out. When he appears to them, his first words are: "Peace be with you" (Jn 20:19).

Imagine the relief: the Messiah they forsook has risen from the dead, and he comes in peace, not judgment. Jesus continues: "Peace be with you. As the Father has sent me, even so I send you" (Jn 20:21).

Why has the Father sent the Son? Jesus came into the world to teach and to heal, to save us from sin and reconcile the world to himself, to build the kingdom and to extend the mercy of God on earth. But how can the apostles, imperfect men as they are, possibly be sent just as Jesus had been sent by the Father? Jesus answers the question: "He breathed on them, and said to them, 'Receive the Holy Spirit. If you forgive the sins of any, they are forgiven; if you retain the sins of any, they are retained" (Jn 20:22-23).

This fulfills the mysterious words Jesus had spoken on Holy Thursday: "Truly, truly, I say to you, he who believes in me will also do the works that I do; and greater works than these will he do, because I go to the Father" (Jn 14:12).

This statement would have been impossible for the apostles to comprehend a few days earlier when Jesus first said it. How could they do greater things than Jesus? But his resurrection and the coming of the Holy Spirit ultimately bring a startling clarity to everything Jesus has said and done.

When the Holy Spirit comes, he transforms the apostles in a powerful way. Up to this point, they have followed Jesus and they have come to trust in him. Now, Jesus unites himself to them in an astonishing way. They will no longer be mere followers. Rather, they will be mystically united to Christ so that they become extensions of him. As he said: "I am the vine, you are the branches. He who abides in me, and I in him, he it is that bears much fruit, for apart from me you can do nothing" (Jn 15:5).

The risen Christ will send his Holy Spirit so that he can live on in his Church. His apostles will extend the kingdom by means of the sacraments of the New Covenant, drawing all who will come back into relationship with God.

Saved by Grace

Nicodemus had come with human faith, and Jesus had

told him that he needed to be reborn in baptism to enter the kingdom. The crowds were fed with miraculous bread and they wanted to make Jesus an earthly king. Jesus told them that they must eat his flesh and drink his blood, calling them to the Eucharist. Now the apostles—who had told Jesus they would follow him anywhere but who had run away in fear —were forgiven and commissioned to go out and forgive the sins of others by means of confession. In short, at each of the three Passovers, the people who came to Jesus were called to the sacraments of the kingdom.

While we must repent and believe, the kingdom comes about not so much by what we do to serve God, but by God working in and through us. Through the sacraments and the Church, Jesus extends his life into the world. What Jesus did once in history in his physical body, he continues to do throughout history through his mystical body, the Church. Liturgy and sacraments are not remnants of the past; they are the very means by which Jesus makes himself present to us today.

Through baptism, we are united to Christ and receive new life—the very life of Jesus. Through the Eucharist we are fed and nourished with the very Body and Blood that won our salvation, the body crucified for our sins and risen from the dead, never to die again. In confession, the sins and failings that will inevitably afflict us on this earthly pilgrimage are healed and forgiven, and we are strengthened for our journey. Jesus accomplishes all of this through his Church.

All other religions are about man seeking God; Christianity is about God seeking and finding each one of us. God is active and alive in the midst of the Church he founded. This point becomes very clear to St. Paul at the moment of his conversion to Christianity.

Paul (also known as Saul), while on his way to persecute the Christians, was struck down to the ground on the road to Damascus. He then heard a voice saying, "Saul, Saul, why are you persecuting me?"

Saul responds, "Who are you, Lord?" And the voice responds, "I am Jesus, whom you are persecuting" (see Acts 9:3-5).

When Saul was persecuting the Christians, he was actually persecuting Jesus himself, because of the intimate connection between Christ and his followers. Saul was acting in sincerity, but he was sincerely wrong about Jesus and his Church. Even today, there are those who, while acting in sincerity, fail to recognize the Church for what it is—the body of Christ—and persecute Jesus by persecuting the Church. Like Saul, they are not condemned, but called to conversion. Jesus has come to offer them more.

The King and His Kingdom

Jesus has established his Kingdom. It is a universal Kingdom, extending throughout the world, and it is an everlasting Kingdom, extending throughout time. Everyone is welcome. Like the first Christians, we must *repent* from our self-centered lives and turn to God. We must *believe* that Jesus is the Holy One of God and that he has the words of eternal life. And we must be *baptized*, reborn of water and the Spirit, so that we can be grafted into the vine that is Christ.

Becoming a Christian means entering into the New and Everlasting Covenant. The seven sacraments of the New Covenant[9] are the lifeblood of the Christian. By means of these sacred liturgical rites, we are grafted into and sustained in the life of Christ. We live the life of Jesus within the context of the visible Kingdom, united under the leadership of the bishops—successors to the apostles. They, in turn, serve in union with the Pope—successor to St. Peter, the prime minister, who holds the keys of the kingdom. We live in Christ and under the care of the queen mother—Mary—whom he has shared with us. And we serve a king who loved us while we were yet sinners, and lives to guide us home, so that when our earthly life has run its course we may come to our true motherland—heaven.

---

[9] Baptism, confirmation, Eucharist, reconciliation/penance, anointing of the sick, matrimony, and holy orders.

CHAPTER 6

A PERSONAL SEARCH FOR TRUTH

We have been discussing the fact that belief in Christ and his kingdom is reasonable. But Christianity is so much *more* than merely reasonable, so much more than a set of ethics. It is a relationship—one that I have come to experience personally. For example, I can offer a hundred good reasons why I married Michaelann, and they are all true, but our love affair is so much more than reasonable. It is romantic; it's love. The same is true of my relationship with Jesus Christ. There are ample reasons to believe and follow Jesus, but this is more than a court case, or a collection of arguments built upon good evidence. It is a drama, an adventure, and a classic love story of a God who loved me and came to rescue me.

Graciously Saved

I did not need to be born in a Christian home for Christ to find me. In fact, I was conceived outside of wedlock by a woman who was not Christian. I began life in one of the most dangerous places on earth in the late twentieth century: a womb.

Yet because of her kindness and heroic generosity—which I will never be able to repay—she saved my life, carried me to term, and gave me up for adoption.

Through no effort of my own, I found myself alive and adopted by a wonderful young couple. My new mother was a Catholic. My new father was a good man who respected my mother's faith, and five weeks after my birth, I was adopted a second time—this time as a child of God, when I was baptized into the Catholic Church. I was too young to know the gift being given me, just as I was too young to understand the blessing of having been adopted into a wonderful home. The Church speaks beautifully of infant baptism when it states:

> Born with a fallen human nature and tainted by original sin, children also have need of the new birth in Baptism to be freed from the power of darkness and brought into the realm of the freedom of the children of God, to which all men are called. The sheer gratuitousness of the grace of salvation is particularly manifest in infant Baptism. The Church and the parents would deny a child the priceless grace of becoming a child of God were they not to confer Baptism shortly after birth. (*CCC* 1250)

A Prodigal

I grew up in this wonderful home, and as a child, I was

surrounded by the love of my parents, and I came to have a strong devotion to Jesus. I remember wishing that I had been born a couple of thousand years earlier so that I could have known him and perhaps even followed him. I never questioned the love of my parents or the love of God. This was a grace many people do not have—and a grace that I squandered as I grew into a young man. While I never questioned the love of my parents or of God, I did not respond to it.

We live in a world that is at war with God, and I became a casualty of that war. I don't ever remember thinking that I wanted to end my relationship either with God or with my parents, but through a thousand choices, I made those relationships impossible. I did whatever I felt like, regardless of whether my parents or God would approve, and to live this self-centered life without discord, I simply concealed the facts from those closest to me. I did not realize that you can't live in relationship if you refuse to live in the truth.

The foundation of a good life is to choose what is good. Life without the pursuit of goodness places you on a slippery slope. Sure, I had rationalizations for every choice, but my life began to slide out of control. Selfishness is like salt water: the more you drink, the greater your thirst. In my self-absorption and sin, relationships with my family and friends crumbled, and God became little more than a childhood memory.

The lie of the world is that the pursuit of pleasure will bring you happiness. Just buy some more things, eat or drink some new product, or find another person with whom you can be intimate, and that will bring you happiness. But you have been made for more. I had pursued personal pleasure, and I found only loneliness. The truth is that only when we pursue goodness will we experience happiness, and it is only when we live in relationship with God, the Ultimate Good, that we experience the joy we were made for. As St. Augustine said long ago, "You have made us for yourself and our hearts are restless until they rest in you."

Reality and Relationships

Following God takes faith, but God has designed this world in such a way that we are reminded from time to time that there must be more to reality than meets the eye. I was in my late teens and in the depths of self-absorption when something happened—my grandfather became ill. We lived a thousand miles away from my grandparents, and I did not think about them very often. How could I, when I was so busy thinking of myself?

Things did not look good for my grandfather, so my mother was planning to go to his side. My father asked me if I would accompany her on the trip. On one hand, it was a free trip to New Orleans. On the other hand, hospitals were really depressing, and spending a couple of weeks alone with my mother was not on the top of my "to do" list. Our relationship had become filled with tension. It is painful to love someone who does not love you back. My mother had given me nothing but love and support, and I had answered her gift with ingratitude. Nevertheless, I accepted the invitation and went with my mom to New Orleans.

When we arrived, I hardly recognized my grandfather; he was frail and appeared to be near death. Racked with pain, his bodily suffering was aggravated by his keen sense of loneliness. He frequently cried out for my grandmother, who had passed away a few years before. I did not know how to talk to him. I remember being paralyzed by the reality of his suffering and impending death. Meanwhile, my mother did what a good Catholic daughter would: she called for a priest. When the priest arrived, my grandfather was not eager to see him, but the priest calmly asked my mother and me for some private time with my grandfather to hear his confession.

When we returned twenty minutes later, the priest was gone, and we found a man transformed. Though the pain was still there, my grandfather was at peace. In his final days he spoke with us, and as he neared death, he looked forward to being with God and being reunited with the wife he missed so dearly. As I sat in that hospital room, I realized that life is a drama, and relationships define who we are. Someday, I, too, would die. What would my life stand for? My grandfather had turned to God, received the sacraments, and discovered peace. Did I believe in God? What had happened to the God I had loved as a child? These were haunting questions for which I had no answers.

Lost but Looking

I knew there was a hole in my life, but I didn't know how to fill it. My sophomore year in college was my first year away from home. I traveled a thousand miles to Louisiana State University, not too far from where my now-deceased grandparents were buried. The famed LSU was a party school, but I wasn't in a party mood. Self-indulgence had proven to be a hollow pursuit, so I avoided the craziness that seduces so many in college.

I was fortunate to draw a graduate student as a roommate. Howard was not only a serious student; he was engaged to be married. He worked hard all week and then went home every weekend to be with his fiancée. During the week, I found myself doing my schoolwork alongside him. On the weekends, I would fill my time playing basketball until I could hardly walk. For weeks, I would return to my room exhausted, my school work up-to-date. But while wild parties raged all around, I held back, sensing that the happiness I longed for could not be found there. One day, as I sat in my room, something caught my eye. There on the end of the bookshelf was the Bible that my mother had given me before I left home. I picked it up and began to read.

I opened up the New Testament and found the familiar figure of Jesus. As I turned the pages, I found myself being drawn into the drama of his life. Now a young man, I remembered that, when I was a boy, I used to wish I could have known and followed Jesus. I had not thought much about him in years. But now, as the days passed, I found myself coming back from basketball a bit earlier so that I would have more time to read the Bible. I was fascinated by Jesus. As I read, it was as if I were watching a movie in my mind. I tried to imagine what Jesus looked like, how he spoke, how the crowds responded to his teachings and miracles. And then, as I was "watching," Jesus spoke these words: "Why do you call me 'Lord, Lord,' and not do what I tell you?" (Lk 6:46).

I felt as though I had been punched in the stomach. As I read the passage, it was as if God had inserted an extra word: "*Curtis,* why do you call me 'Lord, Lord,' and not do what I tell you?"

I put the Bible down and sat dumbstruck. *Did I think Jesus was God?*

Yes.

Then why didn't I do what he told me?

I had no answer.

I have no idea how long I sat there, but after quite a while, I noticed it was getting dark. I stood up and stumbled down to the dining hall for dinner. As I waited in line, someone walked up and asked, "Would you be willing to take a quick survey?" I don't even remember saying yes, but I found a short questionnaire in my hands. I looked down, and to my surprise the first question asked, "Do you believe in God?" Still in a daze, I wrote, "yes." The survey continued, "Do you believe that Jesus Christ is God? Do you believe the Bible is the word of God?"

I was astonished at the timing. If they only knew what I had been pondering in my room just moments before, the survey

takers would have been astonished as well. I answered yes to
these questions as well. It continued, "Would you like to be in
a Bible study?"

Even though my head was spinning, I recognized that this
question was different. If I answered "yes" to this one, someone
was going to call me or come by my room. I didn't go for things
like that. But then I thought, *I need to speak with someone.* How
could I start doing what Jesus wanted me to if I had no idea what
he was asking of me? So I answered "yes," and gave them my
room number.

Sure enough, a few days later, there was a knock on my door.
When I opened the door, there were a couple of pretty normal
guys on the other side. They mentioned that they had received
my survey and were hoping to get a Bible study started. But in
the meantime, they asked, would I be interested in joining them
for a round of golf? Since I enjoy the game and had some time
on my hands, I agreed to join them for a round.

At the course, I met some other guys, and we all headed out
for a round. We all had a good time, and we went out for a pizza
afterward. At dinner they asked me if I would be interested in
joining an intramural football team. Over the next few weeks,
we played golf and football and went fishing. In the midst of it
all, I met some really great guys. One of them, Roy, told me he
was ready to start a Bible study and asked me if I wanted to join.
I thought, *Why not?* I liked these guys and also wanted to get
some answers to my questions.

Under the Mercy

Shortly after we began meeting, I asked Roy if I could speak with him. I told him I really enjoyed these new friends and the Bible study, but I had to be honest: I was a mess on the inside. I told him about my Bible reading and about the verse I had read, Luke 6:46, when Jesus had seemed to challenge me personally to obey him. I believed that Jesus was Lord, but I had no defense for failing to do what he said. In fact, I didn't even know how to start. I told Roy that I had been trying to be a better person so that I could start following Jesus, but all my efforts seemed futile, and I felt hopeless.

In reply, Roy gave me some of the best advice I have ever received. He told me, "Curtis, you will never get your life in order enough to follow Jesus. What you need to do is give your life to Jesus right where you are, and let him reorder it. Jesus is calling you into relationship, not merely to obedience."

He went on to explain that if Jesus rose from the dead, then he is alive and wants to be in a living relationship with me. He told me that I could begin that relationship by turning to him in prayer, asking him to come into my heart as my Lord and Savior, and asking for his forgiveness. That night, in my own words, I prayed the following prayer:

> Lord Jesus, I truly believe that you are God; that you came and died for me. I am sorry for my sins; please forgive me. I desire to be in relationship

with you. Please come into my life as my Lord and
Savior. I desire to live for you and with you and to
follow you with all of my heart, mind, and soul.

Right Relationship

With Christ as the Lord of my life, things began to
change. My entire life began to be transformed. I experienced
forgiveness and the joy of being in right relation with the
God who had created and saved me. I began to meet people
who likewise were seeking to live in relationship with God.
They were men and women of solid character—people who
wanted to become the best that they could be and who were
eager to help me do the same. I began to rediscover meaning
and purpose in life. Even my grade point average rose more
than a full point; meaning in life translated into excellence
in my schoolwork. In a very real way, learning the truth
about Jesus helped me to know who I was. Later, I found
that this was precisely what Pope John Paul II was teaching
as he traveled the world calling men and women back into
relationship with Jesus.

> Man cannot live without love. He remains a be-
> ing that is incomprehensible for himself, his life is
> senseless, if love is not revealed to him, if he does
> not encounter love, if he does not experience it
> and make it his own, if he does not participate

intimately in it. This is why Christ the Redeemer "fully reveals man to himself.[10]

I learned how to talk to God as I would to a trusted friend. I discovered the wisdom and power of God's inspired word, the Scriptures, and I developed a heart for others. My entire focus shifted from pursuing personal pleasure to creating a life centered on right relationships and living in the truth. I developed some of the best friendships I could have imagined and I began learning what it meant to be a loyal and concerned friend. The rest of my college years were the best of my young life, and I desired to continue growing in my intimacy with Christ and others.

During this time, my closest friends were evangelical Christians, and they were (and still are) some of the best people I had ever known. I considered myself a "former" Catholic who was now a devoted Christian, and my greatest desire was to grow in my faith—a desire I pray I will carry with me to my grave. I recognized the authority of Sacred Scripture and desired to conform my life to God's will by faithfully following his word.

I Believe What You Say, but What Do You Mean?

All Christians agree that the Bible is the word of God, and we all agree on what the actual words of Scripture say. Yes, it is true that Catholics and Orthodox Christians have a few

---

[10] John Paul II, *Redemptor Hominis*, 10

more books in their Old Testaments compared to Protestant Christians, but we all agree on the twenty-seven books of the New Testament, and there are no fundamental doctrines that spring exclusively from these missing Old Testament sources.[11] Nevertheless, I began to see that there were many different opinions about *how* to interpret what the Bible says, and these differences troubled me. If there is one God, and he has one Son, and he founded one Church, and that Church has been given all of the truth (see Jn 16:13), why are there so many differences of opinion about what the truth is? How can a modern Christian find the fullness of truth?

Sure, there is some room for differences: "Do you prefer to read the psalms or the letters of St. Paul?" or "Are you partial to the parables or the precepts that Jesus uses to teach the Gospel?" But, other issues seem to offer little room for differences of opinion without compromising the whole Christian faith: "Are you justified by faith alone, apart from works, or does neglect of good works endanger your salvation?"; "Is the Eucharist the literal Body of Christ or is it merely a symbol?"; "Are sacraments like Baptism, Communion and Confession optional or does God expect all of us to receive them?" We all agreed what the Bible *said*, but how could I come to know what it *meant*?

---

[11] The doctrine of purgatory is sometimes mentioned as an example of a teaching that relies upon the "Catholic" Old Testament, but 1 Corinthians 3:15 gives a clear New Testament basis for this apostolic teaching.

The Witness of History

I continued to pray for insight, I listened to many teachers, and I continued to study. I attended a wonderful seminar put on by Campus Crusade for Christ. The lecturer was Josh McDowell, who is a gifted speaker and a well-informed teacher. His particular subject was the reliability of the Bible. Christians form their faith according to the Bible and try to conform their lives to its teachings. The workshops raised the question: *Can we trust that the Bible we have is an accurate representation of what was actually written two thousand years ago?* McDowell presented powerful and compelling proof that the Bible is the most reliable ancient text in the world and that we can have great confidence that what we are reading, while translated into our own language, is based upon extremely reliable copies of the original manuscripts.

The foundation for McDowell's argument was the testimony of history. We can have confidence in the texts because there are many ancient documents, and each bore witness to a common source. The very minor differences in the ancient texts affected less than a fraction of one percent of the text, and no essential doctrine was called into question by these differences. McDowell stressed the fact that these ancient documents were copies created close in time to the originals and that they were well known and honored by the Church as Scripture. The early Christians would have rejected any additions or deletions from the originals.

I began to wonder: If the testimony of history could prove what the Bible *said*, could history also help me discover what the Bible *meant*? If the early Christians faithfully copied the Bible, did they also write about what it meant? A trip to the library provided the first answers to my dilemma. Yes, the early Christians did write books about their faith. Using the logic McDowell had taught me, I applied the test of history to what the Bible meant.

I was shocked. One of the most ancient witnesses was a man by the name of Ignatius of Antioch. His pedigree was impeccable. Jesus had commissioned his apostles to go make disciples, and one of his apostles, John, had discipled Ignatius. Surely, Ignatius' thoughts on the meaning of Scripture would be reliable. Not only was he instructed by an apostle; he was later martyred for his faith in Christ.

To my great surprise, Ignatius believed things that I did not—and made it clear he had received those ideas directly from the apostles. Ignatius laid great stress upon "the bishops" and "the Eucharist." In one particular letter, he wrote the following:

> Those who belong to God and to Jesus Christ—
> they are with the bishop. And those who repent
> come to the unity of the Church. Take care, then,
> to use one Eucharist, so that whatever you do, you
> do according to God: for there is one Flesh of our
> Lord Jesus Christ, and one cup in the union of His

Blood; one altar, as there is one bishop with the presbytery.[12]

My church did not have any bishops, and I had come to think, along with my Evangelical friends, that the Lord's Supper was merely symbolic.

I also noticed that both of these teachings reconciled with the Catholic faith of my childhood. This was troubling because, by that time, I had concluded that the Catholic Church was wrong about many things. My misunderstanding was not unique. In fact, the Catholic Church may be the most misunderstood institution in history. This makes sense since Jesus himself was often misunderstood. The late Bishop Fulton Sheen described this common bias that many have against the Catholic Church:

> There are not over a hundred people in the U.S. that hate the Catholic Church, there are millions however, who hate what they wrongly believe to be the Catholic Church—which is, of course, quite a different thing.[13]

My personal experience made me inclined to agree with my

---

[12] Ignatius of Antioch, *Epistle to the Romans*, ch. 4. Roberts, Alexander, and Donaldson, eds. *Ante-Nicene Fathers, Vol. 1: The Apostolic Fathers, Justin, Irenaeus.* Http://www.ccel.org/ccel/schaff/anf01.v.v.iv.html

[13] *Radio Replies, Vol. I.* Rumble, Leslie, and Carty, Charles, eds. (Rockford, IL: TAN Books and Publishers, 1979), p. ix

Evangelical friends. After all, they were the most faithful people I had ever met. But I could not doubt the faithfulness of Ignatius. I was torn. I wanted to have a shared faith with my friends, but I also saw the need to have a shared faith with this ancient saint, formed by the apostle John.

Something More than Meets the Eye

I began to look around for options. At this time, I could not believe that the Catholic Church was the true Church. From my perspective, there seemed to be so many objections to Catholicism. I thought many Catholic teachings were contrary to Scripture. I didn't know Catholics who seemed to follow Christ the way my Evangelical friends did. So many Catholics were either lukewarm in their devotion to Jesus or even living lives contrary to the teachings of Christ. Indeed, I had *been* one of those Catholics not too long before. Wouldn't the Church Jesus had founded be filled with faithful people?

I continued to pray and read. Ignatius of Antioch had much to say, but he wasn't the only early Christian who wrote books. I began to read others, people known as the "Church Fathers." To my dismay, they spoke much the way Ignatius did. In fact, they all seemed to speak with pretty much the same voice. In the historical church there were bishops, the pope, the Mass, the sacraments, devotion to Mary, and moral teachings that were very recognizably Catholic. Sure, some of these teachings and practices were in seed form, still developing and being elaborated upon. But it was all there. The Church the Fathers showed me was, unmistakably, a *young Catholic Church*!

It really bothered me. How could I disagree with the growing mountain of compelling evidence? But also, where could I find Christians today who had the deep devotion to Christ I had come to experience with my Evangelical friends, but who also held to the historical teachings of the first Christians? Was there a Church that taught all that the apostles taught and was also home to God's faithful people?

As I read the gospels, I began to see something I had not noticed before. The main theme of Jesus' teachings was the Kingdom of God. The first words of his public ministry were, "Repent! For the Kingdom of God is at hand." The Sermon on the Mount spoke repeatedly of this Kingdom. When Jesus was crucified, his "crime" was claiming to be the King of the Jews. More than one hundred times the New Testament mentions the Kingdom. But, there was one aspect of the Kingdom that took me by complete surprise.

In Matthew's gospel, Jesus shares seven parables about the Kingdom, and they reveal something I would not have expected. The parables show that *the Kingdom is a mixed reality*. The first and longest of the parables compares the Kingdom to a field of wheat in which the enemy comes and plants weeds. When the workers realize the problem, they go to the landowner and offer to pull out the weeds. But the landowner forbids them, telling them to let the wheat and weeds grow up together lest some of the wheat be pulled out by accident. He assures them that he will separate the wheat and the weeds at harvest time. This meant that the Kingdom would not only have faithful members but also sinners living side by side, who would be separated only in the end.

In other words, the mere fact that some in the Church were not faithful was not evidence against the validity of the Church. On the contrary, *it was actually a characteristic of the Church.* The question was not, "Are there sinners in the Church?" The real question was, "Are there saints?"

Again I looked to history and around the world. I could find examples of faithful people who were Protestants, like C. S. Lewis and Billy Graham. But I could also see great saints from every generation in the Catholic Church—people like St. Ignatius of Antioch, St. Francis of Assisi, and St. Thérèse of Lisieux. So if there were faithful people in both camps, how could I find the camp that Jesus founded and was faithful to all of his teachings?

Billy Graham and Mother Teresa

I began to look more closely at the great modern leaders. I decided that I would focus on two examples: Billy Graham and Mother Teresa. As far as I could determine, both were devoted followers of Christ. Both led lives of prayer. Both accepted the authority of the Bible. Both had dedicated their lives to bringing Christ to others. Despite these similarities, one was Protestant and the other was Catholic. Mother Teresa, however, held the same teachings that the Early Church Fathers did: she believed in bishops and she spent an hour a day praying before the Eucharist. Who was right? I began to see that both were right—in what they shared in common. This gave me great hope, but it made me come to see something vitally important: *It is possible to follow Christ with great faithfulness even if you do not know all that he taught.* But it is not possible to live faithfully if you knowingly deny Christ or his teachings.

Billy Graham could be a loyal disciple—devoted to Jesus as Lord and Savior, committed to prayer and reaching souls for Christ—but because of a lack of understanding, not know that Jesus was truly present in the Eucharist. What he affirmed was true, but he did not affirm *all* of the truth.

On the other hand, how could Mother Teresa be a loyal follower of Christ if she devoted her life to worshipping the Eucharist *if it were just a piece of bread*?

There is really no middle ground: Either Jesus is present in the Eucharist, and therefore all Christians can and ought to pray to him, or Jesus is not present in the Eucharist and it is merely bread, in which case praying to the Eucharist would be a foolish form of idolatry. This is an issue that only allows one right answer. Jesus either is or is not really present in the Eucharist. The historical evidence proved that the content of Mother Teresa's faith was the same as the ancient Christians. They unanimously confirmed that the Eucharist was truly the Body and Blood of Christ.

Calling Believers to More

I realized there was a biblical parallel for my situation as an Evangelical who believed some of the apostolic faith, but not all. St. Paul met somebody like me when he went to Ephesus and found a small group of early Christians who were faithful but had never heard of the Holy Spirit. When they heard the apostle teach the Gospel, in all of its fullness, they accepted it and joined themselves to the Church in union with the apostles (Acts 19:1-7).

I had accepted Jesus as my Lord and Savior. I lived by the motto, "If Jesus is not Lord *of all*, he is not Lord *at all*." I needed to follow him wherever he would lead me, and to my surprise, he was leading me to the Catholic Church.

Jesus founded the Church through his life, his teachings, his death, and his resurrection. My friends in Campus Crusade for Christ had taught me the importance of making Jesus the Lord of my life. This had to include believing all that he had taught. In fact, our Lord's final words to his disciples were given moments before he ascended into heaven. He gave us his Great Commission:

> All authority in heaven and on earth has been given to me. Go therefore and make disciples of all nations, baptizing them in the name of the Father and of the Son and of the Holy Spirit, teaching them to observe *all* that I have commanded you; and lo,

I am with you always, to the close of the age. (Mt 28:18-20, emphasis added)

If Jesus is truly Lord of everything, then it is incumbent upon all of his followers to accept *all* that he commanded. The true Church must have Christ's continual presence and must proclaim not just *most* of his teachings, but *all* of them. This includes such things as the reality of bishops, who are direct spiritual descendants of the apostles, and Jesus' true presence in the Eucharist.

All Christians agree that Jesus *said* the Eucharist was his body. Matthew, Mark, Luke, John, and Paul all confirm his words. But, all Christians do not agree about what Jesus *meant*. Was he speaking figuratively or literally? The clear, unambiguous, and unanimous testimony of the early Christians (as well as all modern Orthodox and Catholics) was that his words were to be taken literally. And throughout the centuries there has never been a time when saints did not bear witness to that truth. In fact, there is a continual presence of great saints, who loved Christ with all their lives and believed all that he taught.

To this day, I wholeheartedly affirm that we are justified by God's grace through no merit of our own—which is just what the Catholic Church teaches: "Since the initiative belongs to God in the order of grace, *no one can merit the initial grace* of forgiveness and justification" (*CCC*, 2010, emphasis in original).

Likewise, I still believe what I was taught by my Evangelical teachers—that the Bible is the authoritative and inerrant Word of God. I believe this because it is what the Catholic Church has always taught:

> For Holy Mother Church, relying on the faith of the apostolic age, accepts as sacred and canonical the books of the Old and the New Testaments, whole and entire, with all their parts, on the grounds that, written under the inspiration of the Holy Spirit, they have God as their author and have been handed on as such to the Church herself. (*CCC* 105)

I believe, just as my Evangelical friends do, that we are called to evangelize all people—and this is just what the Catholic popes have always taught:

> We wish to confirm once more that the task of evangelizing all people constitutes the essential mission of the Church . . . Evangelizing is in fact the grace and vocation proper to the Church, her deepest identity. She exists in order to evangelize.[14]

But in addition to these Catholic truths that Evangelicalism faithfully preserves, I now know we are called to believe that Jesus is present in the Holy Eucharist, to recognize that Mary

---

[14] Pope Paul VI, *Evangelization in the Modern World*, 14

is our Mother in faith, and to learn from the teaching of the successor of Peter and the other apostles. As an evangelical I learned much of what Christ taught. As a Catholic I have embraced it all. Acknowledging Christ as King means nothing less than accepting his Kingdom—including his prime minster, the pope, and his queen mother, the Virgin Mary—and allowing His sacramental grace to transform every aspect of my life. This is the life of a disciple, to let Christ reign in my life.

The Gospel of the Kingdom

Faithfulness to Christ means being a loyal member of the Church he founded. If we will accept Jesus as Lord and King, we must accept and embrace his Kingdom. Yes, the Kingdom is a mixed reality, with sinners and saints. We must always work for the renewal of the Kingdom, but we are not free to reject the Kingdom that Christ founded and continues to guide. To follow Jesus means to embrace the Catholic Church.

> To reunite all his children, scattered and led astray by sin, the Father willed to call the whole of humanity together into his Son's Church. The Church is the place where humanity must redis-cover its unity and salvation. The Church is "the world reconciled." She is that bark which "in full sail of the Lord's cross, by the breath of the Holy Spirit, navigates safely in this world." According to

another image dear to the Church Fathers, she is prefigured by Noah's ark, which alone saves from the flood. (*CCC* 845)

The duty of a follower of Christ the King is to extend his reign on earth. First, he must reign over our own hearts and minds, for we cannot give what we do not have. Then we must extend his reign to others by sharing the good news of his truth, mercy, forgiveness, and love to anyone we can.

I am grateful to God for the love and witness that my Evangelical Protestant friends shared with me. I hope that all people will come to love the Scriptures. But to truly love the Scriptures, we need to embrace what the Bible *means* and be united with the great Kingdom Christ has established. So it is my great hope and prayer that all people will embrace the true church of the Bible, and become members of the Church that Jesus himself founded, the Catholic Church.

CURTIS MARTIN

Although adopted into a Catholic family and raised in a faith-filled home, Curtis Martin's college years at Louisiana State University found him wrestling with many of the same questions young people are asking today; questions about faith, life's meaning and discovering purpose in the world.

One day in his dorm room, Martin picked up a Bible and began to read the Gospels. In the months that followed, a group of campus missionaries invited Martin to join a Bible study, play rounds of golf, and ultimately, enter into a relationship with Jesus Christ.

From this experience, Martin's vision for FOCUS was born. Today (2009), there are more than 250 FOCUS missionaries serving on nearly 50 campuses across the United States.

Curtis is the President and founder of FOCUS and the author of several books, including "Catholic for a Reason" series with Dr. Scott Hahn. He is also co-host of the ground-breaking show on EWTN, *Crossing the Goal*. In 2004, Curtis and Michaelann Martin were awarded the Benemerenti medal by Pope John Paull II for their outstanding service to the Church.

KEY TO BIBLICAL ABBREVIATIONS

The following abbreviations are used for the various Scriptural verses cited throughout the book. (Note: *CCC = Catechism of the Catholic Church.*)

Old Testament

Gn	Genesis	Jdt	Judith	Hos	Hosea
Ex	Exodus	Est	Esther	Jl	Joel
Lv	Leviticus	1 Mc	1 Maccabees	Am	Amos
Nm	Numbers	2 Mc	2 Maccabees	Ob	Obadiah
Dt	Deuteronomy	Jb	Job	Jon	Jonah
Jos	Joshua	Ps	Psalms	Mi	Micah
Jgs	Judges	Prv	Proverbs	Na	Nahum
Ru	Ruth	Eccl	Ecclesiastes	Hb	Habakkuk
1 Sam	1 Samuel	Sng	Song of Songs	Zep	Zephaniah
2 Sam	2 Samuel	Wis	Wisdom	Hg	Haggai
1 Kgs	1 Kings	Sir	Sirach	Zec	Zechariah
2 Kgs	2 Kings	Is	Isaiah	Mal	Malachi
1 Chr	1 Chronicles	Jer	Jeremiah		
2 Chr	2 Chronicles	Lam	Lamentations		
Ezr	Ezra	Bar	Baruch		
Neh	Nehemiah	Ez	Ezekiel		
Tb	Tobit	Dn	Daniel		

New Testament

Mt	Matthew	Phil	Philippians	1 Pt	1 Peter
Mk	Mark	Col	Colossians	2 Pt	2 Peter
Lk	Luke	1 Thess	1 Thessalonians	1 Jn	1 John
Jn	John	2 Thess	2 Thessalonians	2 Jn	2 John
Acts	Acts	1 Tm	1 Timothy	3 Jn	3 John
Rom	Romans	2 Tm	2 Timothy	Jude	Jude
1 Cor	1 Corinthians	Ti	Titus	Rv	Revelation
2 Cor	2 Corinthians	Phlm	Philemon		
Gal	Galatians	Heb	Hebrews		
Eph	Ephesians	Jas	James		

Made for More

Order Curtis Martin's book in bulk for as little as $2 at DynamicCatholic.com/pbp

Order online or call 513–221–7700.
$2 a copy for orders over 500. $3 a copy for orders up to 499.
Shipping and handling included.

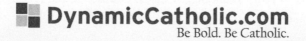

DynamicCatholic.com
Be Bold. Be Catholic.

FOCUS
Vision for Life

11 years. 185 vocations. 400 missionaries.

FOCUS, the Fellowship of Catholic University Students, is a national outreach that sends teams of missionaries to college campuses to introduce students to the love of Jesus Christ and the Catholic Church.

FOCUS missionaries meet college students where they are and invite them to examine the meaning and purpose of their lives. Compelled by the love of Christ, FOCUS missionaries bring a message of hope and truth to a world searching for something more.

How to Get Involved:
- Join a Bible study
- Help with service projects and social outreaches
- Learn to share the Catholic faith and Jesus Christ with others

To join FOCUS or to bring FOCUS to your campus, visit us online at www.focusonline.org.

FOCUS • PO Box 33656 • Denver, CO 80233 • www.focusonline.org • (303) 962-5750

What is the Measure of a Man?

In a culture experiencing a crisis of masculinity, Tim Gray and Curtis Martin's "Boys to Men" is an invitation to delve into the heart of true manhood: growth in virtue, the pursuit of wisdom and the meaning of sacrifice.

In this 8-part Bible study, you'll discover an introduction to the virtuous life and the tools to pursue Christ's radical call to true manhood.

Ideal for use in group or personal study, "Boys to Men" provides rock solid advice on living a Christ-centered life, and leading other men to do the same:

- Live a life of Christian virtue
- Experience the power of authentic masculinity
- Discover God's plan for your life

To order, visit www.focusonline.org or call (303) 962-5750

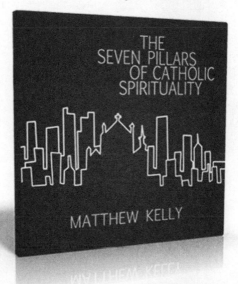
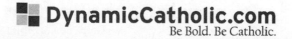

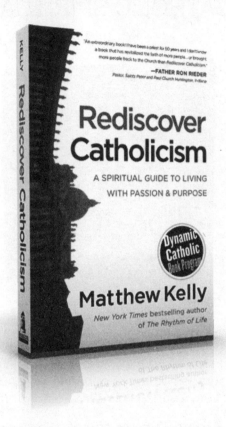
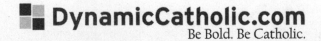